So Young, So Sad, So Listen

So Young, So Sad, So Listen

A parents' guide to depression in children and young people

By
Philip Graham and Nick Midgley

Drawings by
Christine Roche

Foreword by
Philip Pullman

Oh WHERE
Oh WHERE
has my little
spark gone...

CAMBRIDGE
UNIVERSITY PRESS

CAMBRIDGE
UNIVERSITY PRESS

University Printing House, Cambridge CB2 8BS, United Kingdom

One Liberty Plaza, 20th Floor, New York, NY 10006, USA

477 Williamstown Road, Port Melbourne, VIC 3207, Australia

314–321, 3rd Floor, Plot 3, Splendor Forum, Jasola District Centre,
New Delhi – 110025, India

79 Anson Road, #06–04/06, Singapore 079906

Cambridge University Press is part of the University of Cambridge.

It furthers the University's mission by disseminating knowledge in the pursuit of
education, learning, and research at the highest international levels of excellence.

www.cambridge.org
Information on this title: www.cambridge.org/9781911623564
DOI: 10.1017/9781911623557

First published 1995, The Royal College of Psychiatrists
Second edition 2005, The Royal College of Psychiatrists
Third edition published by Cambridge University Press 2020

Printed in the United Kingdom by TJ International Ltd, Padstow Cornwall

A catalogue record for this publication is available from the British Library.

Library of Congress Cataloging-in-Publication Data
Names: Graham, P. J. (Philip Jeremy), author.
Title: So young, so sad, so listen : helping depressed children / by Philip Graham and Nicholas Midgley ; drawings
by Christine Roche ; foreword by Philip Pullman.
Description: Third edition. | Cambridge, United Kingdom ; New York, NY : Cambridge University Press, 2020. |
Revised edition of: So young, so sad, so listen / Philip Graham and Carol Hughes. [Rev. ed.]. c2005. | Includes
bibliographical references and index.
Identifiers: LCCN 2019058636 (print) | LCCN 2019058637 (ebook) | ISBN 9781911623564 (paperback) | ISBN
9781911623557 (ebook)
Subjects: LCSH: Depression in children – Popular works. | Depression in adolescence – Popular works.
Classification: LCC RJ506.D4 G73 2020 (print) | LCC RJ506.D4 (ebook) | DDC 618.92/8527–dc23
LC record available at https://lccn.loc.gov/2019058636
LC ebook record available at https://lccn.loc.gov/2019058637

ISBN 978-1-911-62356-4 Paperback

Contents

Sad, Unhappy Mood

'I used to cry every day for the past year and that made me really physically tired as well ... I feel so negative about everything ... disappointed, sad, angry – just all these unwanted emotions ... I have never been happy with my life, never.'
(Freddy, 17)

A child or young person who is clinically depressed may feel sadness and misery for weeks at a time, with little variation from day to day, although the mood might change during the day. Even though circumstances might alter, the sad mood persists, although they may not always show it. Recognising a persistently unhappy mood may not be easy. A young person may be experiencing a mood change, but not want to admit it. As we will describe, children and young people who are clinically depressed may have other problems, such as anxiety or difficult, disobedient, even aggressive behaviour. It is particularly hard for parents or teachers to recognise persistently sad mood in a child who is being irritating and disruptive. By no means all disruptive, difficult children are clinically depressed, but a sizeable number of them are.

Especially with younger children, the anxiety that often accompanies depression may show itself with aches and pains, especially stomach aches and headaches, which are difficult to diagnose. If a parent is worried there may be something physically wrong with their child, the accompanying depression may be overlooked.

Irritability

'I tend to get so angry . . . Just stupid little things like if someone like for example pokes me for ages, I feel really angry, I don't know it just like little things that get me irritable and then if they keep repeating them then I'll go like literally go mad . . . It's like I shout at them or punch things or just say stuff I don't even like really mean . . . I've even punched a car before.'

(Mikayla, 14)

Although it isn't often thought about as a sign of depression, irritability is now recognised as a core indication that a child or young person is depressed. In fact, depressed adolescents are less likely than adults to complain of feeling depressed, with some studies finding that anger and irritability are the most commonly reported emotional experiences in clinically depressed adolescents.

Children and young people who are disobedient, rebellious, verbally and sometimes physically abusive may also be depressed. It is often difficult to talk to them about depression because they want to keep their veneer of toughness.

If a child or young person who used to get on with other people is starting to lose their temper or become angry for no apparent reason, this can be a sign that their underlying mood is poor. This can be hard for parents and teachers, who may feel that they need to respond to the 'bad' behaviour, and this in turn may make the young person withdraw even more. When children are very troublesome, it is always worthwhile asking yourself if they are not also very unhappy. Just sometimes, showing a difficult child that one has recognised how sad he or she is may provide the first opportunity for real lines of communication to be established.

Lack of Pleasure in Ordinary, Everyday Activities

'I don't really go out that much anymore, I don't really, I don't exercise as I should . . . I can't be bothered, I can't be bothered putting on make-up, even having a bath.'

(Poppy, 17)

Most children and teenagers will sometimes say they are 'bored'. They usually mean they can't find anything interesting to do. Their friends may be away or do not call them or it's raining and they can't get out to play football. Such boredom is not usually a sign of clinical depression. However, it *is* likely to be a sign when a child or young person does have the opportunity to do things they normally enjoy but do not want to participate. That is the time to worry. Friends call around but they don't want to have anything to do with them. They show no interest in PE at school, although this is usually their favourite lesson. If children and teenagers show a change in behaviour like this over a period of some weeks, this is a clear warning of clinical depression.

Disturbed Sleep

'I just lie there, trying to get to sleep ... but my mind won't let me.'
(Mo 11)

This can show itself in a number of ways. Difficulty getting off to sleep, waking in the night and being unable to get back to sleep and waking much earlier than usual in the morning are common. Suddenly sleeping a lot and having difficulty getting out of bed can also be a sign. Persistent, unhappy and troubling dreams or nightmares are less common but may occur. So may sleepwalking and sleeptalking, but they are even less common.

Children vary greatly in the amount of sleep they need and, as they grow, their sleep patterns can vary enormously. How does one know if a child is getting enough sleep? Tiredness and lack of energy during the day are signs of this. On the other hand, the fact that a child will not go to sleep when parents think he or she should is not necessarily a sign of depression or indeed of anything at all being wrong with the child. Some children and teenagers do genuinely have less need for sleep than most. The child who has a lot of energy during the day is probably getting enough sleep, although many parents might wish they saw less of him or her during the evenings!

Changes in Appetite

Some children with clinical depression become very picky and go off their food. Others turn to food for comfort and eat far more than is healthy. Either way, if there is a persistent change of appetite, this is a worrying sign.

Dieting is common among teenagers, and we are all aware of how much pressure there is on young people about their appearance these days. Dieting is not, of course, in itself a sign of depression. It is the child who suddenly does not enjoy food, having usually enjoyed it, who is much more likely to be depressed.

We will discuss anorexia and bulimia (pathological over-eating) as problems that may be associated with clinical depression, later in this chapter. It is often difficult to know whether depressive symptoms are causing an eating problem or whether it is having an eating problem that is making a child or young person depressed. Unhappiness with one's appearance may, for example, arise from depressive feelings that lead to excessive dieting or exercise. Or repeated failures to stick to a ridiculously low-calorie diet may lead to a feeling of failure and depression.

Either way, if a child or young person is showing a persistent change of appetite and attitude to food that is affecting their life, they may have a clinical problem and need help.

Thoughts about Wanting to Die and Suicidal Behaviour

'If I am by myself I might think about how, if I did, I'd kill myself. Like once was like "ah, I might drown myself" so then like I filled up the bath and I was like, but then I thought about it – I didn't think – I was like "ah". I decided to see where life goes for a bit before I try this, so I haven't like tried to kill myself again.'
(Liam, 14)

For nearly all parents, the possibility that their child might wish to die is the most worrying of all the signs of depression, and rightly so. According to an authoritative survey carried out by the Office of National Statistics (ONS), about 1 in 20 eleven-to sixteen-year-olds report having self-harmed or attempted suicide at some point in their lives with about one in sixty reporting this to have occurred in the month before they were interviewed. (That will mean 14 students in a secondary school with 1,000 students on roll.) About 1 in 7 deaths in the fifteen-to nineteen-year age group is due to suicide, with boys about twice as likely as girls to take their own lives. Fortunately, suicide is very much less common under the age of thirteen or fourteen years, but it does occur.

Not all children who have suicidal ideas are depressed. Fleeting thoughts that life is not worth living are quite common in the young without depression. A child who stamps a foot when denied a favourite television programme and says 'All right, I'll kill myself' may just be copying behaviour seen on some other television programme. And if the child is out playing with friends only half an hour later, this is likely to be the case.

Nevertheless, any indication of suicidal intention in young people must be taken very seriously. Recognising that a youngster has persistent suicidal thoughts is often not an easy matter. Numerous surveys have revealed that parents are usually quite unaware of whether their teenage children have these thoughts, and it is not at all uncommon for young people to be able to cover up from their parents even when they have actually harmed themselves. Obviously, if children show depression in the other ways described here, it is important to consider the possibility that they may have suicidal ideas. Remarks by a child or a teenager that they are feeling hopeless or that life is not worth living should be taken seriously. Indeed, persistent hopelessness about the future and a view of the future as bleak and unpleasurable are further signs of depression.

With younger children, their play may reveal how they are feeling. Play with dolls that constantly repeats themes of separation from parents, dangerous or reckless play, destructive play and play that constantly involves life-endangering themes – all these may indicate that even quite a young child of six or seven has suicidal ideas. Of course, a lot of children will be taken up with fantasy figures like one of the X–Men, whose life is constantly in danger, and when deciding if a child's play is really a sign of depression one needs to think about whether there are other signs as well.

It is difficult for parents and teachers to accept that a teenager may be having suicidal ideas. For parents, particularly those who have themselves had suicidal ideas and who are under stress, the additional load of such thoughts in their child may be just too much to bear. For a teacher stressed by demands made, for example, by workload, lesson planning, marking and pressure for teaching groups to achieve high grades, as well as perhaps preoccupied with other problems at home, the thought that a student might be suicidal creates possible responsibilities for action it might be easier not to take. Yet the recognition of suicidal thoughts in a depressed teenager may be a life-saving achievement.

Friends of a suicidal teenager will find themselves in a difficult position if their friend confides their suicidal wishes but swears them to secrecy. Young people sometimes feel that they are the only ones who understand their friend and try to keep things secret. But this is an unfair burden – and possibly a dangerous one. Friends will be doing their best for their depressed friend by letting responsible adults know and not keeping the secret.

Sometimes Friends Are Not Aware

When Alesha, at fifteen years old, took an overdose, her best friend was stunned. 'I didn't know anything was wrong with her. Yes, I realised she had been a bit weepy and unhappy recently, but I just put it down to "that time of the month". When the class heard that she'd tried to kill herself they were freaked out. Some of them reacted by calling her a nutter and then not wanting anything to do with her. But a few of us were really tearful because we were frightened that we would end up doing the same thing, and maybe no one would succeed in stopping us.'

Teachers need to be aware of the copycat effect that sometimes arises following a pupil's attempted or successful suicide. Other pupils' anxieties and fears of not being able to cope can be stirred up by the event, and some may be tempted to as well. Discussions in the classroom can be helpful, and there are many resources available to teachers to help facilitate such discussions (see the Resources section at the end of this book). It is useful to allow time for each child to express feelings about what has happened, about the loss of a school friend and whether they feel guilty that they could, somehow, have stopped it. One should be particularly sensitive with more vulnerable children who may be experiencing similar feelings and anxieties.

Self-Harming Behaviour

'Banging my head against something . . . It's a temporary measure to just continue with my lesson or whatever . . . I sort of do it when I'm feeling like if I don't release something it will keep building up and I might actually do something that would really, really upset my family or friends – so I sort of feel sort of like a mini-catharsis I suppose.'
(Sabrina, 16)

All suicidal behaviour involves self-harm, but, as the example of Sabrina illustrates, not all self-harming behaviour carries a suicidal intent. In particular, cutting the skin has, over the last forty years, become a much more common form of self-harming behaviour. Children and young people who cut themselves, when asked why they do it, usually say, like Sabrina, it is to release intolerable tension.

Although cutting is by far the most common form of self-harm, there are other ways in which children and young people can harm themselves. These include hitting and biting themselves, deliberate scratching, abusing pills, and bone-breaking by reckless falling or jumping. Many, but by no means all, children who harm themselves in these ways are clinically depressed. Anger (often with other signs of antisocial behaviour), loneliness and frustration may be more prominent in how they feel. They are all likely to show low self-esteem.

Sometimes people mistakenly think that cutting in particular is something that girls do, but cutting is increasingly common among teenage boys as well. Social media play an important part here. There are far too many messages on social media treating self-harming as if it were a joke or even something to be admired. In addition, some teachers have noticed that cutting behaviour may show signs of being 'epidemic'. For example, a couple of high-status girls in a class may start to cut themselves and then others follow because they want to be part of their group. Such epidemic behaviour is less likely to be linked to depressive feelings, but should never be dismissed as mere 'copycat' behaviour, as it may still be understood as a genuine cry for help. Furthermore, children who show copycat behaviour like this are also likely to be those with low self-esteem.

Negative Thoughts

'When this all began, I started worrying about everything and that I could never have a positive look on things, like even when people try and cheer me up and when people tell me things are going to be okay, I don't believe them.'
(Shauna, 14)

It has been suggested that people who are depressed have what have been called 'negative automatic thoughts'. These are thoughts that are 'negative' because they are linked with unpleasant feelings, such as feeling sad or bad about oneself. They are 'automatic' because they just seem to pop into people's heads. For example, if someone makes a mistake (as we all do, of course), the thought might pop up: 'everything I do is wrong' or 'if I can't do it 100 per cent right, there's no point in doing it at all'. Then, feelings of being useless and hopeless may follow. Parents, teachers or friends can help by pointing out, for instance, that we all make mistakes; no one is perfect.

Self-Blame

'I feel like my heart is broken ... but somehow I was the one who broke it.'
(Brian, 12)

Depressed children and teenagers sometimes take the troubles of their families, their friends and even the world in general on their own shoulders. They may be perfectionists and have set very high standards for themselves. They may blame themselves for arguments their parents have, for the separation of their parents or for an illness in a brother or sister. Reassurance that they are not responsible may fail to convince them.

Self-blame is not one of the more common signs of depression in younger children, but it does occur. Again, talking with them about the stressful events in their lives may reveal these ideas. With younger children, their playing or drawings may show how badly they feel about their lives, and how they feel they deserve to be punished for things they have not done.

More commonly, there is a loss of self-esteem. The child or youngster just has a very poor view of themselves. Low self-esteem and depression are very closely linked, although they are not identical. Occasionally, a child may have one without the other.

Struggling at School

'I used to just like really enjoy school . . . cos I'm – I get my grades, I get A's all the time and stuff but then like, I just couldn't be bothered no more, like I hated going to school and . . . then I'd get irritated, then I'd just start talking or misbehaving so I can get sent out so I can just go home or whatever.'
(Rihanna, 15)

Although it isn't always seen as a symptom of depression, parents may first notice there's a problem because of concerns at school. A lot of children with depression may struggle at school, even if they used to be bright and popular students. Although some depressed children might be able to keep things going at school, for many it can be a struggle and attendance may suffer. If children are low on energy, have lost motivation or are finding it hard to sleep well at night, then they might start finding it hard to get to school on time or finish their homework. Difficulties with concentration can often go hand-in-hand with other problems, which can make the whole experience of engaging with education an ordeal:

'At school I can never get up so I'm always late for school and come really late – like I would miss two lessons and then I come in, and then when I am in lessons I don't concentrate and then I get really behind on my work, homework and things – I don't really do it.'
(Jade, 16)

Other Signs

In thinking about whether a child or teenager is depressed, the presence of any of the problems described here should be regarded as a warning sign. But there are other issues to bear in mind. Has there been a change in the child's normal behaviour? A child who is happy not to see friends more than occasionally is different from a sociable child who gradually stops wanting to see friends. How is the child's everyday life affected? The child who is functioning well despite the presence of these problems may be less a cause for concern than a child who is, for example, unable to do schoolwork, losing weight or missing school activities.

It is not always easy to distinguish depression from understandable distress. But in some ways, it is not all that important to do so. If a child or teenager remains depressed or distressed, whatever you like to call it, over several weeks, there is reason to be worried and to want to do something about it. Suicidal thoughts and self-harming behaviour are always a major cause for concern, whatever one calls the problem underlying them, and however severe or apparently trivial the disappointment or loss the child has experienced.

Associated Problems

Children and young people who are depressed often have other mental health problems and these may be very prominent, so that the depression is masked by them. If a child has an associated problem with prominent symptoms, depression may be missed unless it is thought and asked about.

Anxiety

The most common associated problem is excessive anxiety and worrying. Indeed, these are so commonly associated that some people think they are part of the same condition. Anxiety states commonly occur by themselves without any evidence of depression. More commonly, though, the two occur together.

Anxiety comes in many different forms. There may be excessive worrying about pretty well everything there is to worry about – parents breaking up, parents getting ill or even dying, not doing well enough at school, being the wrong body shape or just generally unattractive, not being liked by friends – these are among the most frequently experienced worries.

Some depressed children have specific phobias. In younger, preschool children, fear of separation from parents and fear of the dark are the most common. Fear of the separation from parents involved in going to school ('school phobia') becomes more common in primary school as a symptom linked to clinical depression.

As children move into their teens, fear of going out and social anxiety in group situations often occur in those who are depressed. Children who are clinically depressed may also have panic attacks in which they fear they are going to faint, feel they may be dying and suffer physical symptoms like palpitations of the heart. These can be extremely frightening both for the child and for parents.

The anxiety shown by depressed children may also show itself by bodily aches and pains, especially headaches and stomach aches. These may result in visits to the family doctor, who will not be able to find any physical cause for the symptoms. Of course, depressed children may also suffer from appendicitis and various forms of colitis, so it's important that they are checked out to make sure there is no physical problem underlying such symptoms.

Difficult, Aggressive Behaviour

Children and young people who are disobedient, rebellious, verbally and sometimes physically abusive may also be depressed. It is often difficult to talk to them about depression because they want to keep their veneer of toughness, but it is sometimes possible. When children are very troublesome, it is always worthwhile asking oneself if they are not also very unhappy. Just sometimes, showing a difficult child that one has recognised how sad he or she is may provide the first opportunity for real lines of communication to be established.

Chronic Fatigue

Persistent tiredness and lack of energy are important signs of depression. When these are the most prominent problems, a child or teenager may be diagnosed as having chronic fatigue syndrome (CFS) or myalgic encephalomyelitis (ME), or post-viral fatigue syndrome. CFS sometimes follows a viral or flu-like illness. The child shows extreme fatigue after exercise, for example. The problem may be prolonged, lasting weeks or even months. The disorder has much in common with depression – in particular, it often has both physical and psychological components; but fatigue can be a symptom of depression in itself and is not always an indication of CFS.

Parents of children with CFS may feel that the mental health team does not take the physical component of their child's problem sufficiently seriously, because they are using an entirely psychological approach. In fact, most mental health professionals do accept there is a physical contribution to CFS; they also believe that the best way to produce improvement is to concentrate on gradual increase in exercise.

Obsessive-Compulsive Symptoms

These may be shown by excessive checking, for example, to make sure all the doors are locked at night. The child or young person may not be able to get intrusive thoughts out of his or her head. Such symptoms may arise because the child is depressed, or the oppressive nature of obsessional symptoms may bring on depression.

Eating Problems

Another commonly linked set of problems are the eating disorders, especially anorexia nervosa and bulimia (compulsive over-eating). We have already seen how changes of appetite may be signs of depression.

Some clinically depressed girls, and increasingly boys, develop inferiority feelings about their appearance as part of their generally low self-esteem. This may lead to dieting behaviour to achieve a more fashionable body shape. Dieting may become compulsive, so that an eating disorder develops in addition to the depression.

Alternatively, some young people who have developed anorexia nervosa for other reasons may become depressed because they feel trapped in a cycle of failure over their dieting behaviour often accompanied by periodic bingeing.

Self-harm is relatively common in children and young people with eating disorders and, when it occurs, it often arises out of depressive feelings of hopelessness about appearance, social situation and disturbed relationships.

Alcohol and Drug Problems

Finally, and often overlooked because parents are so focused on the way their teenage children are using alcohol or drugs, is the fact that excessive alcohol and drug use may arise because of depressive feelings. It is surprising to some people that the average weekly consumption of alcohol in eleven-year-old British boys is six units and in fifteen-year-old boys is seven units, the equivalent of three and a half pints of beer. Quite a few drink much more than this and the rate increases quite sharply with age.

Many young people just drink alcohol at parties and then only in moderate amounts and there is no reason to think depression plays any part in their alcohol consumption, but this is not the case for a minority. Some may be drinking because they feel miserable and/or anxious. Feeling low is also a physical consequence of consuming alcohol.

The most common illegal drug used by children and young people is marijuana, weed or grass. Occasional use at weekends is unlikely to be linked to depression, but some children and young people are heavy users. They may well feel low and demotivated after using, usually smoking the drug. Their heavy use may also occur as an attempt to cheer themselves up when they are depressed for other reasons.

Young people who drink heavily or who use drugs on a regular or frequent basis may get depressed because they run into financial problems and cannot afford the habits they have developed. Heavy cigarette smoking can have the same effect. Children and young people who are drinking or smoking heavily or are on drugs may turn to petty and sometimes more serious crime, stealing from shops as well as from home. In its most extreme form, this occurs in those children and young people who have been trapped by drug dealers into carrying drugs, especially heroin, from big cities to provincial centres along so-called county lines. Either way, the teenager who is depressed and who also has a drink or drug problem is in trouble and will need help.

Psychotic Depression

If this were a book about depression in adults, we would need to spend some time on this subject. Although some children and young people with non-psychotic depression do suffer hallucinations, especially hearing voices, fortunately, full-blown psychotic depressive illnesses are rare in children and adolescents under the age of sixteen years, but they do very occasionally occur, so we must mention them briefly. Nearly all teenagers show mood swings to some degree, but some get very depressed and then in other phases are unusually cheerful, talkative and energetic. In a small proportion of these, very worrying changes occur.

The main special features are delusions (false ideas that cannot be changed even though they are obviously wrong) and hallucinations (usually hearing voices or seeing things that are not there). These psychotic symptoms are often accompanied by a dramatic slowing up of movement and speech. The child may also refuse, or not be able, to eat. Sometimes these psychotic episodes alternate with unusually cheerful moods of overexcitement and overtalkativeness. This is called a bipolar disorder. However, such 'hypomanic' episodes may not occur, and there may just be repeated episodes of severe depression. The disorder is then called unipolar.

Treatment involves counselling and support, medication and, very occasionally, electroconvulsive therapy. It needs to be emphasised that this type of problem is very rare indeed in those under sixteen years of age. Taken alone, hearing voices is surprisingly common among young people, and not necessarily a sign of psychosis. When the full picture described here does occur, however, it always needs specialist treatment.

In Conclusion

Some words of caution: although clinical depression in a child or teenager may sometimes be best seen as a disorder or even an illness, this is by no means the only way to look at it. Depression in a young person may be a sign that something is very wrong in the family or the school or in the neighbourhood. Social, educational and family perspectives on depression are sometimes more appropriate than seeing it as a psychiatric disorder or a medical problem.

Furthermore, we have described many types of behaviour and feeling states that may be part both of clinical depression and of intense emotional reactions to stress. All children and young people showing these problems need sympathy and understanding. In deciding whether they need professional help, you will want to take into account the circumstances that seem to have triggered the problem, the intensity of the emotional reactions, how long the problems have been going on, whether your child's everyday life is affected and whether he or she seems 'stuck' in their predicament.

Understanding Depression in Children and Young People

Chapter 2

This chapter summarises some of what we know about depression: how common it is in young people, where it comes from and what are the things that research suggests may increase or decrease the likelihood of a young person developing depression. We also explain what we know about the most likely outcomes for those who do experience depression.

How Common is Depression in the Young?

Nothing special. Just one in ten....

Surveys carried out every few years by the Office of National Statistics mean that we have excellent information about the rates of depression in children and young people in the United Kingdom. Because the same methods are used at each point in time, this means we can compare the rates over the years. The last big survey was carried out in 2017.

In 2017, about 1 in 12 children and young people aged five to nineteen years in the United Kingdom had an emotional disorder such as anxiety or depression. About 2 in every hundred five to sixteen year olds suffer from depressive disorders to the extent they would benefit from seeing a mental health professional. Compared to the number of children with clinical depression, significantly more children and young people experience intense emotional distress, usually for relatively short periods of days or a few weeks rather than months. Some of these could be described as on the edge of clinical depression. Problems with anxiety are three times more common than depression.

Depression and Age in Children and Young People

When looking at emotional disorders overall, figures in the United Kingdom suggest that about 1 in 25 five- to ten-year-olds experience clinical levels of anxiety or depression, compared to nearly 1 in 10 eleven- to sixteen-year-olds and about 1 in 7 seventeen- to nineteen-year-olds. When it comes to depression in particular, the rate goes up after sixteen years, so that about 1 in 20 seventeen- to nineteen-year -olds are clinically depressed, and at least twice that number show significant distress. Among certain vulnerable groups, such as young carers or children in care, and for those living in isolated rural areas or in troubled, inner-city areas with high rates of poverty, poor community support and high crime rates, the level of depression may be twice the figures we have quoted.

These figures mean that in a secondary school in a reasonably settled area, with 1,000 children, about 50 children will be depressed in any one year. In a primary school with about 400 children in an inner-city area, about 8 children will be clinically depressed, and double that number will be significantly distressed.

Various factors affect the rates of depression, and these are discussed under separate headings in the following pages.

Differences between Boys and Girls

Among younger children, boys and girls suffer clinical depression to a roughly equal degree. After puberty, the rate in girls is higher, so that by the age of fifteen or sixteen years, it is twice as high in girls as in boys. We aren't entirely sure why this is, and some people think that we just aren't very good at recognising depression in teenage boys. Perhaps this is because boys are less good at expressing their emotions. But there could be physical, perhaps hormonal or genetic reasons for this difference. It is more likely that girls respond to stress with depressive reactions more often than boys do because they tend to be more emotionally involved in relationships and in other aspects of their lives. There are some indications that girls tend to respond to bad experiences with more rumination (going over things again and again in their minds), as well as with more self-blame and self-criticism. This could be one reason why levels of depression among teenage girls are higher than in boys.

Sexual Orientation and Gender Identity

Young people aged fourteen to nineteen who identify as lesbian, gay, bisexual or trans (LGBT) are more likely to have a mental health disorder than those who identify as heterosexual, and this includes depression. For example, one recent study suggested that transgender and gender non-conforming young people were three to thirteen times more likely to be suffering from a mental health condition – most often depression or anxiety – than young people whose gender identify corresponded with their assigned gender at birth (cisgender). It is possible that this higher rate among LGBT youth is caused both by concern about how they are perceived by others and by greater levels of discrimination, victimisation and bullying.

Poverty

There is a link between low income and the rate of emotional disorders, affecting about twice the number of children in families in receipt of benefits than in the general population. Poverty and poor social conditions are not, in themselves, causes of depression. However, children living in families where poor home conditions create stress are more likely to be depressed. Parents bringing up their children in circumstances in which they do not know how they are going to get through the week without getting further into debt understandably have difficulty helping their children through the inevitable stresses and disappointments that life brings.

Health and Special Educational Needs

Children who are in poor general health, or who have special educational needs, are more likely to have emotional problems, including depression. It is particularly children and young people with epilepsy and other disorders of the brain who are at risk. Similarly, children with special educational needs are over twice as likely to suffer from a clinical emotional disorder than those with normal educational ability.

going to be taller or shorter than most people, whether we will develop one of a hundred or more rare diseases such as cystic fibrosis, or less rare diseases such as Alzheimer's disease in old age. Genes also have a variable effect, from small to considerable, on whether we have an increased likelihood of becoming depressed.

The inheritance of a particular characteristic may not be present at birth. After all, puberty occurs around about the ages of ten to fifteen years because we are programmed by our genes that way, not because of events that happen to us. It is quite possible that, though it comes on well after birth, depression is partly genetic. There is now a reasonable amount of information from twin studies and from studies of families suggesting that this is indeed the case for some clinically depressed children. But it will probably only be in occasional cases that genes are the most important cause.

In those cases where genes are important, how do they exert their effects? They affect the personality (as we shall discuss) but they may also alter the way the brain functions in response to stress. A great deal of work has been undertaken to see if chemicals (neurotransmitters) that operate in the brain and the passage of messages between nerve cells are affected in depression. Other work has been undertaken with hormones, particularly steroid hormones, that are known to be affected by stress. So far, no conclusive results have appeared, and the role of biochemical factors and glandular secretions in causing childhood depression remains uncertain but it is highly likely they are of major importance with some children.

Temperament and Personality

One way in which genes can increase the chances of a child becoming depressed is by their effect on moulding the child's personality. Children are born with a given temperament, and this affects how parents behave towards them. For instance, a quiet baby with regular body functions who sleeps and feeds highly predictably will be quite a different baby to care for than a noisy baby who is difficult to satisfy and wakes and feeds irregularly.

If parents feel inadequate, anxious, depressed or unsure of themselves, they may not find a way of dealing with their baby that works for them. On the other hand, they may be experienced parents with adequate support, and rise to the challenge of the more difficult baby in order to help the child feel more secure in the early days. These early patterns of relating to others may have longer-term effects in later life. Children who feel understood and in tune with their environment will have a greater inner security and trust that things will work out in the long run. Those who feel the world is at odds with their own needs could well become more pessimistic.

In later years, as they move into school, some children remain easily upset, cry readily and are discouraged by minor disappointments. Such children may be particularly likely to become depressed, and, even more unfortunately, they may in fact contribute to the circumstances that are likely to produce depression. So, for example, a child with this type of personality may be more vulnerable to bullying at school and thus can be at greater risk for one of the stresses that can act as a trigger for depression.

This is an example of what is now called 'gene–environment interaction', in which the features of a child's personality cause problems for the child, thus creating further stress for an individual who is poorly equipped to deal with it.

Has There Been an Increase in Childhood Depression?

It is common to read in the newspapers about a 'crisis in child mental health', and there is no doubt that mental health problems in children and young people are far more visible today than they were ten or twenty years ago, partly due to some important campaigns to tackle the stigma about mental health and speaking out. There is some evidence that interventions designed to reduce the stigma associated with depression have been especially effective.

So, are children more likely to be depressed now than used to be the case? Research findings suggest that the number of five- to fifteen-year-olds with a mental health disorder in the United Kingdom has risen from about 9.7 per cent in 1999 to 11.2 per cent in 2017, suggesting a real rise in rates of mental health problems. For depression, however, the changes have not been marked, although between the early 2000s and 2017 there was a definite rise in the rate of emotional disorders in teenagers, especially in girls. It seems likely that the increased awareness about depression in young people may be one reason why it seems as if depression rates have risen.

Does Depression in Children Predict Long-Term Problems?

Just a RUN OF
The mill GiRL.

The good news is that many distressed and mildly depressed children can be expected to improve over several weeks or months, especially if their problems are recognised, sources of unhappiness are dealt with and they receive appropriate help.

On the other hand, follow-up studies suggest that more serious forms of clinical depression in children and adolescents (especially those accompanied by marked interference with daily life and persistent suicidal thoughts) are less likely to go away without more specialist help. Although recovery rates are still quite high, there is also a much higher rate of relapse – in other words, the depression coming back again sometime later. Perhaps as many as a half of more severely depressed young people will go into adult life with a high likelihood of recurrence and the development of further depressive disorders from time to time; we also know that among those adults who have experienced depression, more than half say they first experienced depression by the age of fourteen.

Sadly, depression, when it occurs in a severe form in childhood or the teenage years, is often by no means a passing phase. A number of young people with depression, once they have been identified and recognised, may need help over months and years. It goes without saying that their parents and any brothers or sisters will also need support, and it is important for parents to check with siblings of a depressed child about how they are managing, and, if necessary, to include them when seeking professional help. Having a child with severe depression in the family can be a major load on family life.

But there is also plenty of reason to be optimistic. In the chapters that follow we hope to make it clear that there is much that can be done to help a depressed child or teenager, as well as other members of the family. Most children who are distressed or depressed will, fortunately, improve with time, support and sometimes more expert help. Even the most seriously depressed teenager may recover and, with help, perhaps having learned techniques to overcome the problem, may be able to lead a happy and successful life.

What Parents Can Do to Help Build a Child's Resilience to Depression

Chapter 3

Introduction

Like a plant, depression grows because a particular seed (perhaps psychological, such as a loss, or perhaps physical, such as a viral infection) has been planted in soil that is good for growth. The child's genes or inherited characteristics, the child's personality and the child's early experiences can be seen together as the soil in which the seed is planted. Just as both seed and soil are necessary for plant growth (you won't get much plant unless you have both of these), so when we look at depression we need to look at both the seeds – the stresses or triggering events – and the nature of the child at the time these events occur. It would be meaningless to say that one or the other is the cause: both are necessary.

But if depression is like a plant, then parents are also gardeners who can play a key role in creating a culture that helps to build a child's resilience in the face of challenges. In this chapter, we discuss some of the things that parents can do to help reduce the risks of a child developing clinical depression.

What Parents Can Do to Reduce the Risk of Depression

Provide Love, Affection and a Stable Home

All children thrive on love and affection. If they feel they are loved they are much more likely to experience high levels of self-esteem. Feeling good about yourself protects against depression.

Children show their need for affection in different ways. Some, especially in the preschool years, may look especially for physical contact, for hugs and kisses. Others, as they grow older, will know that you love them just by the fact that you show interest in what they are doing and are sympathetic and try to be helpful when they run into trouble with friends or at school.

While for some parents, love for a child comes naturally, for others, this is just not the case. Loving a child, like other forms of love, may have to be worked at, and sometimes it's really hard work, especially when a child is being naughty or attention-seeking when you really want to be giving your attention to something or somebody else.

If you are depressed yourself, it will be much more difficult to show loving behaviour towards your child. So, working out how to deal with your own depressive or anxious feelings is not selfish; it will help you get in touch with your loving feelings for your child.

Some parents feel they can't show they love their children except by giving them the latest expensive toy or article of clothing. This is misguided. Of course, you will want to give your children what you can reasonably afford. But many parents are financially stretched and need to explain to their children why they cannot have the same as some of their friends.

Brothers and Sisters

Most people will tell you that you have to treat all your children the same. Well, you can't because they won't let you. Children are individuals. They have different needs for love and affection and will elicit different behaviour from their parents. This means you have to deal with the common complaint 'It's not fair. Why is he getting more than me?' You may need to explain that you show your love for your children in different ways. Although there is no evidence that older, younger or middle children are more liable to depression, in some families the child's position does seem to be important. Some oldest ones feel less special to their parents when another child is born. Some middle children feel left out and some youngest feel squashed by their older siblings. You can't win!

Promote a Healthy Lifestyle

When one thinks of 'lifestyle' it's usually adults one has in mind. But children have lifestyles too and parents have a major part to play in ensuring their children have a healthy lifestyle. The earlier you start the better, but it is never too late to improve the lifestyle of the family as a whole.

1 Diet

Children who are overweight are sometimes teased or bullied at school, so avoiding this will reduce the risk of your child becoming depressed. When a child reaches the age that they can sit down with you and the rest of the family at mealtimes, make sure these are regular; and if you've not got a habit of sitting down together for meals, see if it is something you can establish. Breakfast is a particularly important meal, so do try to make sure your child gets up early enough to eat it. Snacking between meals should be discouraged and this is easier if there are no easily accessible foods, especially biscuits and sweets.

It is well known that certain foods are healthier than others, and that a good diet usually includes a wide variety of foods. Over-indulgence in foods that are rich in carbohydrates, especially sugar, will tend to make your child put on too much weight.

Remember that children are individuals in the way they metabolise or turn into energy the food they eat. Some children manage to put away vast quantities of food without putting on weight; others seem only to have one extra ice cream and they've put on a pound or two. While the number of calories your child consumes will certainly be the main influence on weight, the metabolism he or she is born with will also be important.

From time to time there is a lot of hype about certain foods or additives making children hyperactive. Mostly there is no basis for this, but if you notice your child seems to go hyper after flavoured, sweet drinks or other foods, it makes sense to cut them out. Don't, however, whatever you do, restrict your child's diet to a degree it affects his or her social life without consulting a dietician or paediatrician.

Once your child reaches the early teen years, especially with a girl, you may begin to worry about her developing an eating disorder, perhaps anorexia or becoming a binge-eater. She will probably know of other girls with one of these problems and may even have an affected friend. Eating disorders are often accompanied by depression. To help your daughter (boys are affected too, but less commonly) avoid developing an eating problem, parents should think first about their own attitude to weight and appearance. Easier said than done, especially if you have a tendency to put on weight, but do try to avoid obsessing about your weight and appearance.

In this day and age, sadly, virtually all teenagers are going to worry about their appearance. You can help by making sure you provide a balanced diet sufficient for a growing child, by making your son or daughter believe they look great even if they don't look like the models that they are seeing online, by encouraging sensible but not excessive amounts of exercise (see 'Activity' section), by discouraging looking at websites or social media that glorify thinness and by encouraging friendships with peers who seem to have a healthy attitude to their appearance. Children who are living healthily are very likely to look healthy.

Finally, on diet, don't forget that, especially in the early years, you are the most important model for deciding which foods and how much your children eat. If you are a finicky eater or a snacker or a binger or are excessively weight-conscious yourself, you can expect your child to develop similar attitudes. If you don't want your child to develop in a similar way, then you will need to change your own behaviour first. As you know, it's hard to change how much and when you eat but knowing how this will affect your child may give you that extra push to give it a go.

2 Sleep

Lack of sleep puts your child at risk of getting depressed. It's really important that your child gets enough good-quality sleep at night to make sure he or she is not tired during the day. Very generally speaking, this means that probably nine to eleven hours are about right for five- to twelve-year-olds and roughly eight to nine hours for teenagers. The best guide to whether your child is getting enough sleep is whether he or she is sleepy during the day.

But not getting enough sleep is not the only reason for tiredness during the day. Lack of stimulating activities may also cause daytime sleepiness. For whatever reason, if your child is sleepy in the day, he or she is more likely to feel depressed, so it's something to watch out for.

Children vary in their sleep needs and if your child is getting less sleep than is recommended but is bright as a lark during the day, there is no need to worry. Children with unusually high sleep needs will, of course, often be difficult to get up in the morning and so will need to go to bed earlier the night before. If children can't get off to sleep, there is no harm at all in letting them read until they feel ready to go to sleep.

The NHS website (see Resources section at the end of this book) provides a lot of helpful tips on promoting healthy sleeping habits for your children. They note that keeping lights dim encourages your child's body to produce the sleep hormone melatonin; and for some children who find it harder to get to sleep, they suggest that you can teach your child some breathing exercises to help them relax before bed. Establishing a regular routine with not too much excitement or stimulation in the hour before bedtime will help your child get off to sleep. A wish to prolong screen time is the most common reason these days for children not getting enough sleep. We discuss under 'Social Media' how to approach this problem.

3 Activity

Physical activity helps to prevent depression. You may have a son or a daughter who is football-mad, who needs no encouragement to be out and about and who falls asleep exhausted by physical exercise just as soon as he or she gets into bed. Because physical exercise is a preventive against depression, if this is the case, your child is less likely than most to get depressed. But there are also many children who need to be encouraged to get out and about. Successful fostering of friendships and the conversation they bring will also mean your child will be more active.

Mental stimulation is important too, so encourage reading and do try to make sure there are enough games, creative materials and puzzles in the house or flat so that your child need never be bored and can develop a capacity for self-expression. Hopefully, you will have time to engage in some of these activities with your child. You may lead a very busy life, but keeping your child active, both mentally and physically, should be high on your priority list of things to do.

Screens can provide much stimulating material. Computer games, played for a reasonable amount of time, can certainly provide significant stimulation; many indeed have great educational content but some are just fun to play and give great pleasure. No harm in that, provided it doesn't go on for too long.

Dealing with Bad Behaviour

There is nothing more frustrating, both for parents and their children, than constant arguments about misbehaviour. For some children, disobedience is the main means of gaining parental attention. This might suggest that they are not getting enough parental attention and, of course, this may be the case. But some children seem to have an inordinate desire for their parents' attention that no parent could reasonably satisfy. Other disobedient children are highly self-willed and will persist in wanting to get their own way to a degree that would test the most patient parent. Incidentally, it may be a little compensation to know that highly self-willed children often grow up to be highly successful because they are so persistent and don't give up easily.

Considerable research has gone into working out what works best when children are disobedient. Standing out as a principal finding is that punishment largely doesn't work. In particular, physical punishment such as smacking, while it may have a temporary effect, is not only illegal in parts of the United Kingdom, but is also ineffective in both the medium and long term, and even in the short term.

A first principle is to avoid situations that bring about disobedience. Probably the best way to do this is to make a point of rewarding good behaviour. It is all too easy to take good behaviour for granted. If your child has a good day or even a good hour, then it's worth showing appreciation with a word of praise and a hug. Then, if it looks as if you are heading for a confrontation, try to work out early on if it's really worth having a battle. You should reserve battles for situations in which you really can't let a child get away with something.

When children are nevertheless disobedient, the first step is to try to work out what it's all about. A principal finding is that largely punishment doesn't work. A child who refuses to get up in the morning, go to bed at bedtime, eat lunch or dinner or clean his or her teeth may be asserting independence or attention-seeking, or may be trying to tell you something. (As a wise colleague once said, there is usually a good reason behind unreasonable behaviour.) Listening to your child and a little bit of experimenting may give you the answer. If you are successful in distracting your child onto another activity this would suggest attention-seeking is at the root of the problem.

As a first step, ignoring the difficult behaviour is the most promising approach. Of course, you can't do this if it would expose the child to danger. You can't let your child run into the middle of the road. But there are many, more minor forms of disobedience you can safely ignore.

Time-out is another well-studied tactic. Sending your child up to his or her room with no screens or other distractions for a defined period of time, perhaps ten minutes for a preschooler and half an hour for a child in primary school, will sometimes act as a deterrent for further misbehaviour.

Whatever line you take, it is important to establish as consistently as possible that particular forms of misbehaviour will always have consequences that are undesirable for the child.

Increasingly, there are parenting workshops available where parents can share experience and get advice in groups about how to handle difficult behaviour. Ask at your local GP health centre if there is one near you.

Special Individual Times

Most parents lead very busy lives, usually having to combine what may be stressful work and earning money with being a parent. You may be financially stretched, not knowing how you are going to be able to buy food to put on the table, let alone pay for a holiday. Indeed, you may not have had a holiday for years. This means you may sigh at the thought of giving special time to a child, especially if you have more than one. But it really is something you need to give priority to. Just ten minutes a day of your time, every day, can make your child feel special and valued.

What you do during this time should be something your child would like to do with you. This probably won't be sitting down and having a chat about what is troubling him or her though just occasionally it might be. Instead your child is more likely to want to play a game or look through old photos or have a cuddle and listen to some music, or go for a walk to a nearby shop.

During this time, both phones and TV should be off. Any interruptions should be ignored. Try it and you will find it worthwhile. And, if it makes your child feel special, this will lower the risk of him or her becoming depressed.

Special Family Times

Your family may consist of just you and your child or there may be a partner and a number of children. Either way, spending time as a family engaged in some activity will give you all a sense of togetherness that will pay off when one or more of you is under stress and needs more support. It may be playing a game or going on an outing to the local park for a picnic or, if you are lucky and can afford it, going on a family holiday. Whatever it is, it will give your child a sense of belonging that will protect against depression.

Fostering Friendships

Good friends are supportive and protect against depression. Your child is likely to start mixing with other children at the age of two or three. Gradually friends will become more and more important influences on his or her life, so that by ten or eleven, friends may well be more important influences even than you, in forming their attitudes and behaviour. So, it's desirable for them to make good friends who are loyal to each other, encourage each other, can have a good laugh with each other but can also confide their feelings without fear of betrayal.

Making good friends may not be easy for your child, but you can help by making sure your child's friends feel welcome when they drop round. You can also help with your child's friendships by giving advice how to stop seeing friends who your child has realised are not good influences. Groups of friends may fall out with each other and, if your child feels he or she can confide in you, you will be able, with your greater experience, to help work out what to do. Remember though that your child's view of what is happening may not be totally accurate and you may need to help him or her see how others are seeing a situation.

Although school is the place where most children make friends, fostering friendships outside school can be very important, especially if things at school are tricky. Such places as sport clubs, drama and theatre groups, church or youth groups and cubs, scouts, guides and brownies are worth exploring. A child needs to feel part of the wider community and if school is a distance away, joining something local may be very beneficial. These spaces can also give your child a chance to be someone different from who they are at school, if the classroom isn't their favourite place.

The quality of your child's friendships is one of the most important factors in whether your child is at risk of becoming depressed. So do cherish your child's friends as well as your child.

Choosing the Right School

Parents, building on dreams of academic success for their children, may decide they would like them to have a head start in reading. So, they might begin to make them start practising writing and recognising letters or words round about the age of three years. This may be a rather futile waste of time, better spent in play, but there isn't anything harmful in it provided the child enjoys doing it. When a child shows he or she really doesn't want to engage, then it is sensible to get on with something else that is more fun.

When planning to send a child to nursery school, helpful friends may say, 'Oh, you must send her to such-and-such a school, because it has by far the best academic record.' It is pointless to argue with friends who take this point of view. Just ignore their advice and bear in mind that academic success is not the best reason for choosing a nursery school. If you want to avoid your child getting academic anxiety and depression, try to choose a school that is right for him or her. This is likely to be a place where the teachers want to get to know the children as individuals, where he or she will make friends, preferably local friends, easily, where parents feel welcomed if they are troubled. The school will be interested in promoting academic achievement in all its pupils, not just those who are very bright; and will care about the children's emotional and social well-being as well. It will be especially concerned with those with special educational needs.

But pushy parents are not the only source of academic pressure. Teachers, friends or other children (maybe via social media), other relatives and, above all, your child himself or herself can be the main source of pressure. All schools nowadays are under pressure to achieve good results in order to maintain their funding; or teachers' pay or jobs may depend on the children in their class achieving certain grades. This can create a toxic atmosphere in schools, where pressure is felt by all to succeed. Some children and young people can't stop driving themselves on even if they are top of the class already. You should try to be aware when this is happening and do your best to help your child resist such pressure.

Social Media

Screens have a bad reputation when it comes to children's well-being.

True, they have been and are responsible for much distress in children and young people. But before we condemn them out of hand, we should remember just how much learning in school and out of it is digital. It's not just access to knowledge that is on the credit side of social media. Many websites have really useful, positive ideas about making and keeping good relationships with others. For some children who, for one reason or another, have problems with making friendships, screens provide a wonderful opportunity for socialising.

Further, time spent on the screens is time not spent on other, perhaps less desirable activities. Since screens came on the scene, alcohol consumption in the young has gone down, as has illegal drug use. There has been a dramatic reduction in teenage pregnancies since screens took up more teenage time, though improved sex education and wider availability of contraception have also been important. Much antisocial behaviour, though not knife crime, has reduced. This may or may not be because of the increase in screen-time. The digital world, like the real world, is complicated.

All the same, there are harmful effects of screen use. It has been linked to a significant amount of misery and unhappiness in children and young people. For previous generations of children, coming home meant being free of peer pressure; now there is no escape at home. Overuse is the main problem, though there are others. Thirteen-year-olds who spend more than ten hours a week on their screens are more than twice as likely to report being unhappy than those who spend less time. Heavy users are more likely to be depressed. Girls are on their screens more than boys, but heavy use is just as bad for boys. Heavy users lose valuable sleep. Children and young people who are on their screens for more than three hours a day sleep for fewer hours and get more depressed. The obesity epidemic affecting children these days has been put partly down to inactivity arising from screen use.

What can parents, teachers and children and young people themselves do to keep screen use within reasonable, healthy limits?

As a guide, parents might ask themselves these four questions.

- Is the screen time of your child uncontrolled?
- Does screen time interfere with what your family want to do?
- Does it interfere with sleep – best gauged by the presence of tiredness in the day?
- Does snacking go on constantly during screen time?

If you are able to answer 'no' to all of these, you are probably on the right track. If you can't, then here are some tips how to get there.

- Start a negotiation with your child by listening to what he or she thinks would be a reasonable amount of time spent on screens.
- If this seems too much, then make your points about interference with family life, sleep, etc., and ask your child how this could be better. Listen to the answers.
- If you want to help your child to cut down, then work out a plan to achieve this together.
- Be firm about screen removal an hour before sleep-time. Make sure that little blue light is off and not adding to your child's difficulty in getting off to sleep.
- Up to the age of twelve or thirteen, phones should be left with parents when children go to bed. Up to about this age, you should know the lock code for their phones.
- Until they reach this age, when their need for privacy makes it no longer appropriate, it is reasonable for you to check their phones and online browser history on a regular basis.

- Be consistent in sticking to the rules you've established.
- Be a model yourself in your use of screens. For example, if you say no screens at family mealtimes, then this means you too.

It is not just the amount of time on screens that is linked to misery, unhappiness and depression. What children and young people watch is equally important. This is where screen safety comes in. What can teachers, parents and children themselves do to protect the young against watching stuff that is upsetting, depressing or otherwise harmful?

With this in mind, sites to avoid are those that promote changing body shape by dieting, medication or other means; those that discuss means of self-harming; and porn sites.

Other screen activities to be avoided are sharing inappropriate images (no need to describe what they are!); getting into intimate conversations with people you don't know; being a victim of or responsible for cyberbullying.

This may not be easy. Again here are some tips how to get there:

- If at all possible, don't allow yourself to be persuaded into buying a smart phone for children under twelve or thirteen years. A phone that can make and receive calls will be quite good enough to keep your child connected with friends and with you and the family.
- After discussion and listening to your child, put on as many parental controls as you can. But don't just assume that having parental controls in place will keep your child safe, as many children quickly learn how to get around them.
- Continuing a dialogue with the child is important with the use of all forms of technology. Talk with them about the potential risks and ask your child what sort of stuff he or she finds upsetting and work out together how this can be avoided.
- Watch 'borderline' suitable sites together and discuss which might be OK and which not.
- Explain how difficult it is to identify people you get into intimate conversations with online, and how easy it is for people to pretend to have quite different identities from those they really have.
- Encourage your child to report harmful sites and threatening or seductive conversations and offer to help them with this.
- Talk to your children about what self-care is and what it might mean for them – encouraging them to be aware of their moods and emotional states and helping them to identify things that they can do to help themselves to feel better at times when their mood is low. Set up good habits that will then support them through their teenage years and into adulthood.

In this chapter, we have discussed how parents can create the conditions that make it less likely that their children will become depressed. In the next chapter we describe how parents can help their children when, as inevitably happens, they face particular stresses in their lives.

4

Helping Children Cope with Common Stresses: What Parents Can Do

In the previous chapter we discussed some of the things all parents can do to help build children's resilience and reduce their chances of developing depression. But there are also some specific stresses that are known to be associated with depression in children and teenagers. When children suffer from depression, it is always important to think of the events that might have triggered the problem. In some children, the stress that has brought on the problem will be obvious; in others it will be far from clear. In this chapter, we focus on six of the most common stresses experienced by children and young people (experiences of loss; parental conflict and separation; academic pressure; bullying and online abuse; gender identity issues; and physical ill health), and discuss what parents can do to help children who face such difficulties.

For obvious reasons, numerous stresses are more difficult to cope with than just one. The more stresses a child is experiencing, the more he or she is likely to become depressed. Sometimes your child might not show that they are feeling stressed directly, but its effect may come out through physical complaints. If you suspect your child is suffering from physical symptoms that you think might be due to stress, then it is always a good idea to take him or her to the GP to rule out any physical cause.

Experiences of Loss

Whatever the problems a child with depression may be facing, a sense of loss is almost always part of the picture. The world is not as it should be. A sense of well-being has been lost. In fact, experiencing loss is an essential part of ordinary growth and development. It can often be the spur to change and psychological maturity. As children and young people move on from one stage of life to the next, they have to lose something of the current stage. If they do not let go, they cannot move on. For a child, going to school for the first time may be exciting, stimulating and open up new social relationships, but it also brings with it the loss of the all-day familiarity of home and closeness to parents. Similar losses occur throughout the lives of children and young people, when, for example, they become sexual teenagers and lose their sexual innocence. In fact, the sense of loss accompanying progress in our lives remains with us throughout the whole of our existence.

What is most important in enabling children and young people to cope with loss is the experience that there are secure, trusting relationships available for support and encouragement. If a child (or adult for that matter) feels basically confident and hopeful in relationships, losses in the 'real', external world can be coped with, even if there is still sadness or grief.

We all become distressed and some of us will become clinically depressed when we are faced with significant losses and disappointments. Children are no exception. As adults, we are aware that the degree of distress we experience in relation to a loss depends on its emotional significance. The same is true for children and young people. The problem for parents is that, especially with younger children, it may be difficult to know how significant a loss has been. As a parent you may be surprised at the extent of upset a loss produces in a child because you have not appreciated its emotional significance. Alternatively, you may be surprised how apparently unscathed a child is by a loss that seemed to you likely to be devastating.

Let us take, as an example, a teenager who has lost a close friend whom they have known since going to nursery school several years previously. In thinking about how upset such a child might be, parents must ask themselves –

• Why has the friend been lost?

If she or he has had a serious illness and died, this will obviously give a different meaning to the loss than if the child has moved away to another school or neighbourhood, or there has been an argument between the two.

• How close was the relationship?

Did the two do everything together, or was this a friendship just based on an occasional contact?

• How many other friends does the teenager have?

The child whose only friend has moved away is in a different position from a child who has five or six other children with whom she or he is friendly.

• Was there a sexual component to the relationship?

It is going to be more difficult for a teenager to lose a friendship in which there was some degree of physical attraction and, perhaps, a physical relationship.

• Is there any 'unfinished business' in the relationship?

For example, did the two have the opportunity to say goodbye to each other? Or did your child only find out that his or her friend had disappeared on returning to school at the beginning of a new term, maybe because the friend had moved to another town during the school holidays? Were there any unresolved arguments when the children last saw each other? If so, perhaps your child has an idea that the friend went away because she or he was angry.

• **What, if any, opportunity will there be for contact in the future?**

Are the two going to stay in contact or speak via Facetime or other forms of social media? Would that help the child cope with the loss?

A similar set of questions might be asked if a child is depressed following a different sort of loss, for example, of a parent (through separation or death), a brother or sister, a grandparent or other relative, a friend, an acquaintance or a pet.

The only way you are going to find out about the answers to these questions, all of which are important to understanding the emotional significance of the loss, is by thinking about what you already know and listening to your child. We shall discuss some of the key skills in listening well in the next chapter.

The experience of loss is a central component of depression. What are the other, more specific stresses? There isn't a great deal of evidence on this, but recently a number of surveys have been carried out in which teenagers and younger children suffering from depression have been asked why they think they have been affected in this way. Listening to what they say has been illuminating. They mention a number of stresses of which three are especially prominent. These are: family problems of many different types; pressure to do better academically or in school subjects; and bullying and the effects of social media. In the following sections, we describe these stresses in more detail. We also suggest how parents, teachers and children and young people themselves can avoid such stresses or deal with them when they arise, as inevitably they sometimes will.

Parental Conflict, Domestic Violence, Separation and Divorce

All parents have times when they don't get along together. Arguments are a normal part of relationships between parents when they are trying to work out how to face challenges. Indeed, there are times in most marriages when a couple really dislike if not hate each other. You can't love someone deeply and live together without getting seriously upset, irritated or fed up with them from time to time. There are two main ways in which couples show their negative feelings for each other – open hostility and silent tension, often with periods of not speaking. For children of all ages, these normal expressions of disharmony and disagreement are threatening to their well-being. When they hear their parents shouting at each other or not speaking, they may well feel anxious their parents are going to separate and they will lose one or even both of them.

There are three common reasons why parents fall out with each other – money, sex and disagreements about the care of their children. Often arguments about the care of children centre around one parent believing the other is too soft or too hard in disciplinary matters. Issues over the amount of pocket money, the level of help the child should be giving in the home, at what time a teenager should be expected to be home when out in the evening, the appropriate degree of pressure over homework – these are all common reasons for disagreement.

When parents argue or stop speaking to each other, they don't, in general, want to frighten or upset or depress their children. They can achieve this best by keeping their disagreements to times when their children are not around. Children who witness arguments are more likely to be distressed than those who don't. All the same, even if you are successful in this, inevitably children will be aware of parental disharmony. On most matters, but certainly not on all, it is helpful if parents communicate with their children at an appropriate level what their disagreements are about. You won't want to talk about disagreements about your sex life. You might want to say something about money matters, especially if money is tight, as it usually is, and your children's lives are affected. You might want to talk as a couple to your children about this, but not if this merely sets off another argument. When you do talk to them, it's important to give both points of view and not to try to recruit your children to your side; it is also important to make clear that the arguments are not their fault, and to listen and understand how your children are experiencing these arguments. Though most children do try to intervene when their parents argue, they are less likely to develop emotional problems if they don't take sides.

Even though the separation of parents is always difficult for children, most recover well from the experience. There are a number of factors that reduce your child's chances of developing emotional problems if your marriage is rocky. It is helpful if there are one or more adults outside the home in whom they can confide, so you should encourage such relationships. If your child has an activity outside the home that he or she finds particularly rewarding – a sport or a hobby or a school subject, for example – this reduces the risk of an emotional problem developing, so this is something else to encourage. And children of disharmonious marriages do better if they get on well with brothers or sisters who can be mutually supportive, and don't feel they have to choose between their parents. So, try to make sure your children get on together by rewarding them for cooperative activities and by doing things as a family as suggested in the previous chapter. Children will model the relationships they make later on in life on how they have seen you sort out your differences.

If arguments and tension come to dominate your marriage, the question of a separation, even divorce, may arise. This is a common scenario. In Britain, about one third of parents with children separate or divorce before their children reach the age of eighteen years. Although separation and divorce of parents is linked to depression in children, so is being brought up in an unhappy home with parents constantly at war with each other. There isn't an easy answer to the question whether it is better for children if warring parents stay together or part. You have to take into account the quality of relationship each of you has with your child or children, how well you are both going to be able to keep contact with them, and how the almost inevitable financial changes will affect them and you.

You will want to make sure your child does not blame himself or herself for the break-up. Many children develop fantasies that it is they who have been the cause of the problems between their parents. Even if arguments over childcare do loom large in your disagreements, do remember it isn't your child's fault if you can't agree what to do.

Whatever happens, do keep negotiations between you over who is to look after the children and money as friendly as possible. Make sure you don't bad-mouth your partner in front of your child however much you have come to dislike him or her. You do need to talk to your children about what arrange-ments are being made for them and why. You also need to listen to what they think should happen. But do not give them the responsibility for decisions. Even though you will want to take into account what they say, such decisions are up to you.

Where there is domestic abuse or violence in the home, this is almost certain to have a negative impact on children, although different children may respond in different ways. A 2017 report by the Royal College of Psychiatrists, looking at the impact of domestic abuse on children and young people, suggests that younger children are likely to become anxious, and may express this through physical symptoms, such as bed-wetting or tummy aches. The report suggests that older boys are more likely to display challenging and aggressive behaviour themselves, whilst teenage girls may be more likely to turn inwards, becoming anxious and depressed and sometimes expressing this distress through eating disorders or self-harming behaviour. Children who have witnessed domestic violence and abuse may sometimes find it difficult to go to school, because they are worried about the safety of their abused parents; and children of all ages can experience post-traumatic stress disorder, which may show itself through nightmares, flashbacks or other physical symptoms. If you as a parent are involved in a relationship where such violence or abuse is taking place, it is important that you seek help, not only for your own sake, but also for the well-being of your children. Further information about useful organisations can be found in the Resources section at the end of this book.

Academic Pressure

In the previous chapter, we discussed how you might go about choosing the right school for your child, a school that would minimise his or her chances of becoming depressed. One of the criteria we suggested was that teachers would not put too much pressure on your child. Remember, however, that a certain amount of anxiety is necessary for learning to take place. Many years ago, two psychologists, Yerkes and Dodson, worked out that there was an optimal amount of anxiety for each task. Too much anxiety and the child would be too stressed to take anything in. Too little anxiety and a child couldn't be bothered to learn. Nowadays, in most schools, the risk is that children are given too much anxiety about academic success, and this is not good for their emotional well-being.

Here are some signs your child is under too much academic pressure:
- Complaining schoolwork is too hard
- Difficulties handing in homework on time
- Reluctance to go to school
- Headaches, stomach aches, rashes or other unexplained physical symptoms, especially marked on Sunday evenings or on days when particular subjects are taught
- Sleep problems, nightmares

The first thing to do if you feel your child is showing stress related to academic pressure is to listen to what he or she thinks about this possibility. Listen to what your child has to say about which subjects he or she is finding too difficult or too easy, which teachers he likes and which he or she finds unsympathetic, to what degree he or she is preoccupied with how other students are doing compared to themselves.

Keeping up a good relationship with your child's school and teachers is one of the most important ways you can safeguard against your child becoming depressed. So try not to miss any opportunities to talk to teachers. Children's behaviour at school is often very different from that at home. If you suspect your child is depressed or anxious, do arrange to talk to someone at the school, probably your child's teacher, about it. Your child may not want you to do this, so you may need to try to persuade him or her that it's really necessary. You do need to see the teacher even if your child objects. Work out with your child if he or she should be present.

Transition points (e.g. starting a new school or moving to secondary school) can be particularly difficult for young people. It can also be harder to get a good sense of how your child is coping with school life when they move to secondary school and are seen by many different teachers, rather than just one.

Don't be surprised if the teacher says your child is not showing any problems at school even if you are having a terrible time at home. That happens. Similarly, at a school event for parents, a teacher may express serious worries about your child when, as far as you are concerned, there have been absolutely no problems at home. Try not to get offended and take seriously what the teacher has observed. You need to work together to help your child over problems whether they are occurring at home or at school or in both settings. In any event, you will need to work out with the teacher and your child what can be done to help. This may just mean reassurance the child is doing fine or giving more or less homework. It's really important, however, not to fill every moment of your child's life with educational activities so there is no time to relax.

Bullying, Including Cyberbullying

Bullying using social media or cyberbullying is probably the most common threat on the Internet. It may occur on a social media site such as Instagram or on text messages or emails or in an online chatroom. Although there are many positives about social media, including the possibility for online support, fun and companionship, unmonitored activity can mean that your child may be persuaded into online gaming, risking money way beyond his or her resources. Your child is very likely to face abuse if they are in a group which, as is unfortunately often the case, is preoccupied with gossip and appearance. Obscene language is the norm in online abuse.

Other forms of online threats include sexting with images of sexual behaviour. Your child may be approached by a stranger with initially harmless messages striking up a friendship, eventually leading to suggestions to meet offline. Such grooming may be leading up not only to meetings but to offers of payment for sending nude photographs or images of sexualised behaviour.

The NSPCC (website address in list of Resources) has suggested various signs your child may give that he or she is subject to online abuse. You should be alerted if he or she:

- Is spending a lot more or a lot less time than usual online, texting, gaming or using social media
- Seems distant, upset or angry after using the Internet or texting
- Is secretive about who they're talking to and what they're doing online or on their mobile phone, or
- Has lots of new phone numbers, texts or email addresses on their mobile phone, laptop or tablet.

The NSPCC suggests the actions you should take. These include:

- Listening carefully to what your child is saying
- Letting them know they've done the right thing by telling you
- Telling them it's not their fault
- Saying you'll take them seriously
- Not confronting the alleged abuser
- Explaining what you'll do next
- Reporting what the child has told you as soon as possible

We would add that, in consultation and in agreement with your child, you may well feel you need to take other action such as helping your child leave the social media site to which he or she is subscribing, changing email address or communicating with the school about the problem. All schools have safeguarding procedures to deal with cases where a child is suspected of being the victim of abuse.

Although bullying on social media (cyberbullying) is now as common as traditional forms of bullying, these still occur far more frequently than they should. Some children are still subjected to physical or verbal aggression. It's more likely to be physical if boys are involved and more likely to be verbal aggression (calling names and spreading untrue stories) if it's girls. Victims may be harassed because of their ethnicity or physical appearance, because they have a disability, or because they are too successful academically and regarded as 'nerds'. The principles of dealing with offline abuse are the same as those you should use with abuse that is online.

Many black, Asian and minority ethnic children in the United Kingdom experience racism, and this is also a form of bullying. Parents can help their children confront racism by listening to their concerns, asking about their experiences, relating such experiences to events to which they themselves have been exposed and supporting their concerns. Where racist abuse has occurred at school, it is important that the school knows about this. All schools have very firm policies on this matter and the great majority try their very best to make sure no racism is tolerated among its students.

Childhood Maltreatment, Including Sexual Abuse

It is now understood that abuse and maltreatment take many forms – including bullying or being a witness to domestic violence, as well as neglect, emotional and physical abuse or child sexual exploitation. In almost every case of significant clinical depression in adults, research suggests that some form of abuse or trauma was probably experienced in childhood, either physical, sexual, emotional or a combination. Some research has suggested that this is because childhood sexual abuse can produce long-term dysregulation of what is called the HPA axis (a key part of the central stress-response system in humans), and that this can make abuse victims more vulnerable to depression later in life, especially when faced by stress.

In children, the effects of sexual abuse may show themselves in a number of ways. For younger children, symptoms of post-traumatic stress (such as panic attacks) or inappropriate sexualised behaviour are most common, whereas for teenagers, the impact may more likely show through depression or substance misuse. Family environment – meaning the level of support and understanding that the child is offered to cope with their trauma – makes a significant difference to how the abuse may affect children in the long term. That is why it is so important for parents not only to protect their children from sexual abuse, but also, when it does occur, to get professional help to ensure that they can support their child as well as possible, to minimise the negative impact that such experiences will have.

A number of children who have been identified as abused will have been moved into local authority care. These are especially likely to suffer from depression as a result of the often-frequent changes of parental caretakers they have experienced. Foster parents and those working in local authority children's homes need therefore to be particularly aware of the increased need of children in their care for specialist help.

Gender Identity Issues

Round about the age of ten or eleven years, most boys and girls, though far from fully sexually mature, will recognise that they are physically attracted to people of the same or opposite sex. This may come as a confusing experience, especially if they are experiencing same-sex attraction, and have grown up in a culture where this is not widely accepted. They may feel they cannot confide in their parents or their friends. They will often obtain information on the Internet but may not find this very illuminating. For many, this time of life and these feelings may be very confusing. Lack of confidence about the future may lead to depression.

As your children move through their primary school years and start to ask questions about sex and where babies come from, it can be helpful to tell them early on that, although most boys are attracted to girls and vice versa, this is not always the case. You may be in a same-sex relationship yourself, or be able to point out same-sex couples among your acquaintances to illustrate this fact. In 'normalising' gay or lesbian relationships, you will help your children if they do turn out to be homosexual, and, if they don't, they will be more likely to be accepting of difference in this respect among their friends. Incidentally, the fact that children know about homosexuality is in no way likely to influence their sexual preferences.

Some children are not comfortable with their biological gender and others, a small but important minority, are sure a mistake has been made about their gender. Some of these will grow up gay and others may be transgender. Not surprisingly, confusion about gender may lead to great feelings of unhappiness and even clinical depression.

Some parents may think that their child is unhappy with his or her birth gender if they start wanting to dress in clothes of the opposite sex. But in the preschool and primary school years, cross-dressing may only be very temporary, lasting a few weeks. If it persists, you can open the subject of gender up in conversation with your child. You know he likes dressing up as a girl, you may say. Does this mean he would really prefer to be a girl? Or vice versa. Or it may be that the child is quite happy with their gender, but also enjoys cross-dressing.

Alternatively, one of the teachers at your child's school may approach you and say your child wants to be known by the name of a child of the opposite sex, or has identified as non-binary. Again, you will need to listen to your child and how he or she sees himself or herself. At this point, you may want to consult an expert in what is now known as 'gender dysphoria' or discomfort with birth sex. Where needed, you can get advice from your GP on how to get a referral. The important principle is that your child knows that you will carry on loving and supporting him or her whatever gender is chosen.

Physical Ill Health

Children and young people with problems with their physical health are more likely than others to develop clinical depression, though most of them do not. There are various pathways to depression linked to physical health.

- After a viral illness, maybe even just a nasty cold, some children become depressed for weeks at a time. More commonly, it is glandular fever which is followed by a prolonged period of tiredness and feeling low.
- Some children with chronic physical problems, like asthma or diabetes, become depressed, perhaps at least partly because of the fact they face more challenges and cannot lead such fully active lives as others without disabilities.
- Children and teenagers are particularly likely to develop mental health problems if they have a physical condition affecting their brain function. So, children with

epilepsy are particularly vulnerable as are those who have neurodevelopmental problems such as learning difficulty and autism.

Remember that, in a depressed child with a physical condition, it may not be the physical condition that is causing the depression. There may be family problems completely unconnected with the health of the child that are upsetting. Alternatively, it may be bullying by other children or the need for frequent admissions to hospital that are more important stresses than the physical illness itself.

Although you may not be able to do anything about your child's physical health condition, the development of emotional problems in children with a variety of physical disorders may be more preventable. It is always important that you listen to your child's concerns; they may well not be the same ones you have. Having listened, discuss with your child at an appropriate level the nature of the physical problem and why it has come about. Children are likely to be as interested in causes as you are. You may well be very anxious about your child's condition and what it means for the future. Your anxiety will be communicated to your child whether you like it or not. It is likely that your child will be anxious about many of the same things as you are. Sharing realistic anxieties may be helpful to both you and your child.

If the presence of the physical condition means that your child's schoolwork may be affected, for example by the need to attend hospital departments or clinics, you will want to let the school know as soon as possible. Similarly, if your child is on medication that may affect concentration or learning, the school will need to know.

Children with physical health problems may have more difficulty than others in making and keeping friends, so you may need to be more active in encouraging friendships than you otherwise might. Friendships do protect against emotional problems, including depression. And try to make sure the fact that you have a child with a physical problem does not dominate your life to the extent you lose your own friends. If you get depressed, the chances of your child getting so too are increased.

Coping Skills and Protective Factors

When a child has to face a disappointment or a stress, she or he is not just a passive individual taking what comes without the ability to do anything about it. Children and teenagers respond actively to bad experiences in order to try to master and overcome them. These 'coping skills' help to explain why some children do not become depressed, even though faced with terrible adversity. Similarly, some children faced with adversity have positive things going for them in their environment, and if these protective factors are present, they lower the risk of depression.

Helpful coping skills include the ability to confide worries to friends and family members, and the capacity to deal with one problem at a time rather than be overwhelmed by a mass of difficulties. Children who have a particularly good relationship with one or both parents, who have someone outside the immediate family, such as a grandparent, in whom they can confide, all are less likely to develop depression when stressful circumstances strike. Just as some children have personalities that make them vulnerable to depression, so others have resilient personalities that mean they are more likely to survive troubling times without becoming depressed.

At the end of this book, you'll find information about online resources, including some that are related to self-care and building resilience. There are lots of things that you and your child can be doing to help develop helpful coping skills. For example, for some people taking time to learn breathing techniques that can be used in times of heightened anxiety is beneficial. Children can learn how to quiet a racing mind by taking time out in a busy day, valuing moments of stillness in their lives. Even something as simple as colouring, listening to music or doing a jigsaw puzzle can help. In recent years, there has been an increasing interest in 'mindfulness' as a way of helping to build resilience against stress and anxiety, and although these ideas were first introduced for adults, there are lots of good apps and online resources showing how children and young people can practise mindfulness in a way that can be both enjoyable and helpful.

The protective factors and coping skills enjoyed by children and teenagers are important because they sometimes give clues as to how best we can help them under stress. Reinforcing natural strengths is often a better idea than trying to invent completely new methods of treatment to deal with weaknesses.

Understanding the role of stress in depression is quite complicated if we try to produce a scheme that fits all children. The diagram below is an attempt to bring all these factors together. You will see how some factors push the young person towards more serious depression, while others enhance resilience. But, of course, no diagram can do justice to the richness involved in the life of one particular child.

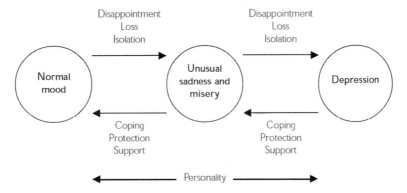

In this chapter, we have described how parents can help their children cope with the stresses that they may face in their lives. But do remember that some children become depressed even though their parents have done everything they possibly could to avoid this happening. In the next chapter, we discuss how parents can be helpful when their children do become depressed.

Chapter 5

When a Child Is Depressed: What Parents Can Do

If you think it is likely that your child or teenager is indeed suffering from depression, you will first want to try to work out why. Often parents are concerned that this is their fault, or that they are somehow to blame for their child's depression. Or you may be worried that something has happened in your child's life to cause the depression which they haven't told you about.

In some cases of child depression, there may be an obvious trigger, either physical or psychological. Your child may have recently experienced one or more of the stresses described in the previous chapter and indeed may be saying that this accounts for the mood change. Or they may have had a viral infection with depression following on from this. More often, the situation is less clear-cut. Instead, there is usually a mixture of reasons, perhaps accumulated stresses. In many cases, neither you nor your child may have any idea at all why this depression has occurred. Furthermore, although expert help may result in much better understanding, it may be that it is never quite clear why the depression occurred in the first place, even, as is very likely after a few weeks or months, your child has improved and is back to normal.

Even if it seems pretty clear what has caused the depression, it may not be at all easy to work out what you and your child can do to change things. Clearly you can't do anything about a viral illness that has now been and gone away. And let's be realistic, often the stress or stresses which seem to be linked to a child's depression can't be changed. Maybe parents have separated; father has another family and has lost interest in his first children. Maybe one of you has a drink problem it is turning out hard to overcome. Perhaps the child has a serious physical illness that is chronic, or even progressing. When such stresses are ongoing and your child's mood persists, all the other ways of helping we will describe here – listening, keeping up the support, sharing feelings and so on – become even more important. Some people find helpful the so-called serenity prayer. You may already know it. It goes: Grant me the serenity to accept the things I cannot change, courage to change the things I can, and wisdom to know the difference.

Indeed, whether or not you can do anything about underlying causes, there is a great deal you can do to improve the situation. To begin with, it will be helpful if you accept what you cannot change. If your teenage daughter is bereft and has developed all the signs of clinical depression because her longstanding boyfriend has 'dumped' her, this is a fact of life. She may want her boyfriend back, but you cannot make him return to her. If your young son has become depressed after he has been wrongly accused of sneaking on a friend and been rejected by his group of friends, you can't make them accept him again or right the wrong he has suffered. It is important that you both accept what you cannot change and acknowledge that your child is indeed depressed. Progress can begin from here.

Listening

Listening to children sounds so simple and obvious, but sometimes it is the quality of the listening that counts more than anything. It is, in fact, rather difficult to listen to children (or people generally) in distress. There are many reasons why children do not get heard in everyday life. For example, in school, they may be overlooked if:

- They are quiet and withdrawn
- The class is too big and troublesome
- Teachers are too tired or worried themselves.

Parents may find themselves overlooking depressed children if:

- They are too wrapped up in their own problems (perhaps death of a relative or friend, marriage problems, how to make ends meet)
- They feel helpless and useless in the face of someone else's despair
- They are just too busy
- It is too upsetting to think about
- Their child does not want to confide in them in order to protect them against getting upset.

So, it is important to look at yourself, to ask whether you are hearing your child's distress and to think about what could be done to help you to listen better. Caring for ourselves enables us to care for our children. As a parent, are you depressed yourself? Support, help, advice and even treatment for parents are important aspects of helping children. It is important not to feel that a child's problems are all your fault, as this, too, may be a block to your listening in a positive way.

Aspects of Listening

Try listening with the heart and not just the ears. Imagine the child's distress by relating it (in your mind only) to periods of distress in your own life, remember how that felt, and think about how your child's experience may be similar, or different, to your own.

Do not belittle the child's unhappiness. You may think your child is just drawing attention to himself or herself. But behind every attention-seeker is a real problem. Perhaps the child needs to dramatise in order to ensure an audience. If the child does not feel you are taking the problem seriously, you run the risk of the child heightening the drama, and perhaps acting in a self-destructive way.

As a parent, if you think your child is attention-seeking, you need to ask why she or he needs so much attention. What is it that this child is trying to draw attention to?

Listening to your child can take time. If speaking to your child, it may help to minimise external distractions, turn off your mobile phone and find a private, secluded room or go for a walk and talk while you're on your way. Shoulder to shoulder listening is often more productive than face to face. Sometimes talking whilst a shared activity is taking place that both of you enjoy can help too – such as walking the dog, baking or doing a jigsaw. Do not allow interruptions – these will make the child feel that the problem is just a burden for you and that you do not, after all, have the time and patience to listen properly.

Tips on Listening

- Do not recount your own worries or upset the child
- Do not tell stories about other people's problems
- Let the child see that you take his or her problems and worries seriously, however trivial you may find them
- Do not attempt to cheer the child up with phrases like 'come on now, it's not the end of the world' or 'it may never happen' – it may just feel like the end of the world to this child, since she or he feels that 'it' has already happened
- Do not give your child the idea he or she is to blame
- Children feel heard and understood if you summarise what they have said by repeating or putting what they have said in another way. Sometimes, if they find it difficult to verbalise, it may be helpful to comment on how they look (e.g. 'you do look upset' or 'I can see how difficult it is to talk about this').

Sometimes when a child is finding it hard to talk, a simple hug can speak volumes. Some children like cuddles and hugs, and actively seek them out; others may be more reticent. Either way, never underestimate the importance of showing your child you love them and care for them, both in words and through your actions.

Drawing and Play

Younger children may find it too hard to talk about their feelings. It can be suggested that they draw whatever it is they are feeling or are worried about. Younger children may express themselves with the help of toys, such as families of dolls and a dolls' house, puppets or toy animals. With younger children, just sitting and watching your child play can often tell you a lot about what is going on for them.

Offering Hope

Given that despair and hopelessness are features of depression, it is important to keep hope alive for the child. It may help to suggest:

- That these feelings will eventually pass
- That there are ways they can be helped, either through talking or by referral to specialists
- That even when depression is ongoing or recurrent, there are still ways to manage the condition and minimise the impact that it has on their lives. One can learn to live *with* mental health conditions, in the same way that one can live, and even thrive, with other ongoing health conditions.

Try to Change Negative Thoughts

Negative thought patterns (i.e. always seeing the worst) are a common feature of depression. For example, after a dispute with a friend in school, the child might say, 'See, no one likes me – I have no friends.' It might help for parents and teachers to examine the 'evidence' of this with the child. 'Didn't Amy ask you to her party last week?'; 'When I picked you up from school, John and Sally said goodbye to you.' It helps to ask the child to try to think about similar situations and provide their own 'evidence' too. As we shall see in the next chapter, this is an approach used by psychologists in so-called cognitive behavioural therapy. But parents can take a similar line. One should not try to prove the child's beliefs wrong; instead one tries to get the child to examine the evidence for his or her negative thoughts. Hopefully this will result in your child realising there is no real basis for them.

Provide Practical Help

Although accepting what you cannot change is an important principle, if it is possible to change whatever it was that brought about the depression, then certainly, in cooperation with your child, you can take appropriate steps to achieve change. More likely, there may also be practical things that will help, such as arranging for friends to come around, or planning and going on an outing

But, do not forget, some problems you think cannot go away may be helped to disappear. Not so long ago, for example, many schoolteachers felt helpless in the face of bullying. They said there was nothing they could do – 'boys will be boys', 'girls can be pretty horrible to each other', etc. But now all schools are expected to have an anti-bullying policy, and much more is being done to prevent this unpleasant aspect of school life.

Keep in Touch

Try not to allow the child to withdraw. This is difficult to achieve without being intrusive. We all know the sullen, uncommunicative teenager who insists that things are all right and tells you to go away. However, you should:

- Keep an eye open and keep watch at a distance, if that is all they will permit
- Persist in expressing your concern from time to time, and reminding them that you are there to listen and talk whenever they want
- Not allow yourself to be fobbed off.

If you continue to be worried, get further advice from a teacher, GP or other professional.

Establish and Maintain a Support System

In your role as a parent of a depressed child or teenager, do try to make sure that both you and your child have a supportive network around you. Your child will have had friends and may not want to see them. Maybe try yourself to maintain contact with them and perhaps their parents so that, as your son or daughter improves, they can re-establish contact. The teachers at your child's school need to remain in touch whether or not he or she is attending.

You will need support just as much as your child. Do keep family members and your friends in the picture and accept help and support from them if it is forthcoming. Even though you may have feelings of shame and failure about having a depressed child, do be honest with those whom you trust and who you know care for you, so that they can be helpful. This will be more difficult if they don't know what is going on. Try to take the time to explain what is going on to family and close friends, especially those with whom the child is likely to come into regular contact. Low mood, reluctance to get involved or take part in activities that they would have done before could be considered as rudeness and a careful explanation will alleviate misunderstanding and prevent the risk of added stress. Family and friends may not have come across depression before and have little understanding and, just as one would do with a physical disability, a detailed explanation can help all those involved. With something obvious, such as a broken leg, everyone understands that special allowances will need to be made. So sometimes it is important to make an explanation of the fact that, while mental ill health may not be as visible as a broken leg, your child is still unwell, and special allowances may still need to be made.

Using the Internet

There are many websites and helplines available for parents of depressed children and for the children and young people themselves. We list those we think are most likely to be helpful in the Resources section of this book. In general, these are of high quality. You should have no difficulty in filtering out those that are merely trying to attract you to take your money for quack remedies. It may be more difficult for your child to filter appropriately. In particular, some websites for teenagers go into great detail how to self-harm as a means of releasing tension. You should try to discourage use of such material. Without being judgmental, try to keep up an open discussion with your child about what kind of websites they are accessing, and help them to think about what information may be helpful or unhelpful.

Your child may have difficulty in talking to you about how he or she feels and may wish to use a helpline. There is no disgrace involved if your child wants to talk to someone outside the family, so encourage this, though do bear in mind the advice in Chapter 3 about how to help your child avoid making contact with harmful individuals via social media.

Confidentiality

Sometimes children will tell you, or another trusted adult outside their family, of their depression (or suicidal feelings) and insist that this remains a secret. This poses quite a dilemma. How much should this confidentiality be respected; to what extent do parents have a right to know about their child's difficulties? It is good practice on the part of health care professionals to involve parents and carers as much as possible in discussions, but the confidentiality of young people also needs to be respected. If the problem is serious or if a child is at risk of suicide or self-harming, there is an expectation that parents will be informed, as long as doing so would not increase the risk to the child (e.g. if parents themselves are abusive and a cause of the child's suicidal feelings).

However, in less worrying situations, it may be possible for, say, a teacher to see a child a few times without informing parents in order to understand the problem better. It may be that poor communication with the parents is, in fact, part of the problem and this can be improved as a result of talking to the child confidentially. Teachers should be doing this within the framework of their school's safeguarding policy, and if things come up that make them worried about your child's well-being, they should be liaising with you about that, to help ensure that your child can be kept safe.

Maintaining a Healthy Lifestyle

In Chapter 4, we described how to ensure your child has a healthy lifestyle as a means to build up resistance against depression. If your child is depressed, paying attention to diet, sleep and activity remains important. Indeed, there is some evidence that taking regular exercise improves depressed mood as much as medication. A depressed child or young person often loses interest in keeping fit and active, so is going to need even more encouragement than others in this respect.

Seeking Professional Help

It is important to know, however, when the techniques listed here are not sufficient and the child needs specialist help. Professional help should be sought when:

- The depression does not lift after 2 to 3 weeks
- There is significant interference with daily life
- There is severe disturbance of sleep and eating patterns
- Suicidal thoughts or wishes are expressed

How to Get Specialist Help

If the problems are occurring mainly at home and do not improve, then the parents' first port of call should be the family doctor. Most family doctors nowadays see emotional problems in children and teenagers as part of their job, although obviously some are going to be more interested than others (that is true of all professionals). Your doctor will hopefully want to see your child and have a chat with him or her, either with you or separately. If your child does not want to go to the doctor (and this is not at all unusual), then you, the parent or parents, should go anyway to discuss the situation. You may be in need of help so that you can continue to cope, and your doctor may be able to provide assistance here. Your doctor may also be able to direct you and/or your child to a counsellor, available under the NHS at the practice, or help you to access support that is offered by local charities or through school. They may also make a referral to specialist services, and we will discuss this more in the next chapter.

If a problem in school has been identified by teachers, parents or by a child, there often needs to be a get-together with everyone (and that 'everyone' includes your child) involved in deciding what to do. It will often be helpful for the child to be present from the beginning. Sharing of information in this situation is nearly always going to be useful. If whatever is decided does not prove helpful enough, then a referral should be made, either to the child and family psychiatric clinic, or, if the problem is mainly to do with learning difficulties or behaviour in the classroom, to an education well-being practitioner or educational psychologist attached to the school. In recent years, it has become much more common for there to be a child and adolescent mental health professional working in the school at least part-time, and every school should have one member of staff who is responsible for the emotional well-being of all children. This makes referral to child and adolescent mental health services (CAMHS) much easier as the professional in the school is very likely to have good contact with the local clinic.

When Professional Help Isn't Forthcoming

It is possible, though much less likely than it would have been even ten years ago, that your family doctor is not helpful. Some doctors still don't believe children can suffer from depression and others are very negative about psychiatrists and psychologists. If this is the case, and you feel sure your child needs professional help, then ask to see a different doctor, or make direct contact with CAMHS. You should be able to find contact details on the Internet. If you are still having difficulty in getting appropriate help, then contact a charity like Young Minds, the charity that is especially concerned with children and young people with mental health problems. It is very likely they will be helpful. (For details about helpful contacts and resources, see the Resources section at the end of the book.)

If your child's teacher or Head of Year is unhelpful, then you should make an appointment to see the Head Teacher. Schools do vary in the amount of help that is available for emotionally distressed students, but most do have a number of ways of supporting such children.

Most CAMHS clinics have waiting lists, sometimes quite long waiting lists, though they are also likely to have a priority system for urgent referrals. If the waiting time seems unreasonable, it's worth contacting your child's school to see if they can get your child to be seen earlier. Alternatively, as we've mentioned, many schools now have mental health professionals and counsellors working on the premises. This may be the case with your child's school.

After seeing you and your child, the doctor should listen, give advice and support and, just occasionally, prescribe medication. Often there will be a need for further appointments to see how the problem is progressing. If, after several weeks, the problem is no better or even seems to be getting worse, then your doctor will probably suggest a referral to the local CAMHS (discussed in the next chapter). This may have been considered earlier if the problem is severe. If your doctor does not suggest a referral, then you can ask for one yourself.

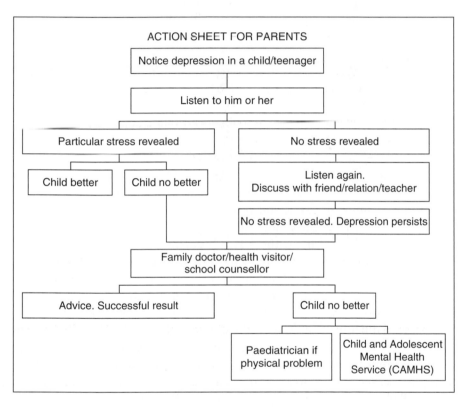

Getting Professional Help: A Guide to Services for Children and Young People with Depression

In the United Kingdom, all those involved with supporting the physical and mental health of children and young people are expected to take into consideration the guidelines produced by the National Institute for Health and Care Excellence (NICE). NICE's most recent recommendations on the treatment of depression in children were published in 2019, and include a lot of helpful advice, mostly based on good research evidence.

As part of their general guidance, NICE suggest that all children with depression, and their families, should be provided with good information from any professionals they come in contact with, and that all professionals should seek informed consent for any decisions about treatment. They also make clear that 'all services should provide written information or audiotaped material in the language of the child or young person and their family or carers, and professional interpreters should be sought for those whose preferred language is not English'.

When it comes to treatment, the NICE guidelines recommend what they call a 'stepped care' approach to helping children with depression, which is about recognising the different needs of children and young people with depression and the different responses that are required from services. It includes the idea that we are all (parents, teachers, professionals) responsible for recognising depression in children, and that when the depression is mild, it is best managed in a community setting. It is only when depression is more severe that it is best to offer treatment in an outpatient, specialist mental health team. If the young person's depression is unresponsive, recurrent or there is an indication of psychotic depression – and especially when there is a real risk to the safety of the child or young person – then NICE recommends that inpatient care should be considered.

Specialist services for child and adolescent mental health problems have different names. In the past they were sometimes called 'family consultation clinics' or 'child guidance clinics' but these days they are known as Child and Adolescent Mental Health Services (CAMHS). Some are situated in hospitals, while others are attached to health centres or are on school premises.

Who Works in CAMHS?

In most CAMHS clinics there will be a number of different child and adolescent mental health professionals. Usually there will be at least one clinical psychologist, psychiatrist, nurse and social worker. There may also be a child psychotherapist and/or a family therapist. These professionals differ in their training and backgrounds. But despite these differences, their skills overlap a good deal. They will all have had training in how to assess emotional problems and in counselling of parents and children. They will all have well-developed skills in listening and in picking up clues about what might be going wrong by careful observation. Often, they will also be skilled in a number of different types of treatment, including psychotherapy with individual children and parents, setting up behavioural programmes or family therapy.

As well as these shared skills, they will all have particular responsibilities and interests. Psychologists often have special skills in assessing learning difficulties and in devising behavioural programmes such as those described in the section 'Cognitive Behavioural Therapy' coming up. Child psychiatric nurses will have a background in mental health nursing and will often be particularly skilled in behavioural management and in working with families in the home. Occupational therapists may also be part of the clinic and can be helpful on advising about activities and practical strategies for getting better. The child and adolescent psychiatrist, who is a qualified doctor, combines knowledge of the emotional and behavioural problems of children and young people with a medical background. Child and adolescent psychotherapists have had a long training in individual child psychotherapy and will have special skills in understanding the 'internal world' of the child. Social workers, who are sometimes part of CAMHS, are generally known for their role in child protection, and this is part of their work, but they will mainly be concerned with improving relationships in the family. They also have special knowledge of the benefits system that may be helpful. Family therapists specialise in observation of the way family members interact together and in trying to intervene helpfully as a result of their observations. There may also be other therapists such as art or music therapists, or health professionals called mental health workers or child well-being practitioners.

What Happens When Your Child Is Referred to CAMHS?

First, there may be a waiting time and, depending on where you live, this is likely to be between one and three months. However, most clinics have an emergency procedure for cases that clearly cannot wait, or they may do an initial assessment before putting your child on a waiting list or suggesting a different type of help. To save time, the clinic may ask you to provide some information on a questionnaire before you first arrive. They may also ask permission to contact your child's school, so that by the time of your appointment, the staff have some idea about your child's progress and behaviour in school.

Different clinics work in different ways, so your first contact may be by phone, or it might be in the form of a letter. Often families are worried by the first appointment letter, which may request the attendance of the whole family, or at least (depending on who is in the family) you and your child together. You may feel that the clinic is suggesting you are to blame in some way for the child's problems. In fact, clinic staff are trained to understand and not to blame. Although it is up to you to decide who should attend, it can be very helpful to have the whole family's views of the current difficulties to help assess the young person and the situations in which the problems occur.

When you arrive, the member or members of the clinic staff who are seeing you will introduce themselves and explain how the assessment will be carried out and how long it will take. Some clinics use one-way screens or video equipment, either for training purposes for staff attached to the clinic who are learning, or because it is felt to be a good way to have more than one view of the problem. If it is intended to use either video or a one-way screen, this will be explained to you and your consent will be necessary for its use. You may find this approach too prying and you have every right to withhold consent. However, it can be helpful to those who are trying to understand and help your child and family.

A big difference between the clinic and the general practitioner is the greater amount of time available at the clinic, hopefully an hour or more. Further, the staff have had special training in listening to children and parents talking about their problems, so they will have greater experience in assessing children and young people who are unhappy and depressed.

Their approach should involve working with the child and family in a collaborative way. They may begin by wishing to see the whole family together and then the child or young person separately, before seeing the parent or parents on their own.

Most professionals working in CAMHS have a favoured approach. They may, for example, put most emphasis on seeing the whole family or they may mainly work with the child or adolescent alone. Some will be more interested in dealing directly with the symptoms or complaints, and others in exploring what is going on underneath. All should want to spend time listening and trying to understand the predicament in which the child and family find themselves. While, in some circumstances, most professional staff will prescribe or recommend the prescription of tablets, they will probably not want to recommend medication until they know the child better and have explored other possibilities.

Towards the end of the assessment, the members of the clinic staff who have seen you are likely to explain how they see the problem in the first instance and what they suggest for the future. They should include you in these discussions, although they will also need to respect the autonomy and wishes of the child, so that any decisions are made in a shared way, rather than just being told by the professionals what you should do. Some families are offered advice on the spot and it is suggested that they return only if problems persist. However, if the depression is quite severe, the staff are quite likely to think it would be a good idea to see the child or adolescent on a number of occasions for treatment following the assessment visit. They may, for example, explain that rapid change is not to be expected but they are hopeful that, with treatment, there could be some improvement over the next few weeks or months. They will write to your family doctor or whoever has referred you, giving the results of the assessment. They may wish to be in touch with the school again.

When Charles was eight years old, he was referred to CAMHS by his family doctor because he had been having stomach aches and headaches for the past six months. As a result of these pains, he had missed school for most of these six months. He had been previously seen by a paediatrician, who had done some blood tests, all of which had turned out to be normal. The paediatrician thought the pains were psychological and had given some advice, but the pains and school absence had persisted.

The clinical psychologist who saw Charles, an only child, and his parents had previously written asking for a school report. His teachers said there wasn't too much they could say about him as he had been absent so much, but, as far as they could see, he was a pleasant, quiet boy who had no problems with the school work, though he had rather few friends. The school expressed concern about his absences, which they had been told had a physical cause, and asked to be kept in the picture.

The psychologist saw Charles and his parents together to begin with. She noted that Charles sat very close to his mother and that his father sat a little separately. The psychologist asked the family to explain how they saw the problem and whether they thought coming to the clinic was a good idea. Charles's mother immediately began to speak. She said that she had not been at all keen to come to the clinic. She was still pretty convinced the problem was physical. She talked for quite a long time about how 'normal' Charles was and how there was no one in the family who had had nervous trouble. It turned out, however, that since the onset of the pains Charles had really been very easily upset, tearful and sleeping poorly. He was unable to settle to anything, even computer games that he normally enjoyed. The clinical psychologist obtained a full account of the development of the symptoms and of other aspects of the background to the referral. It was, however, difficult for her to bring the father or Charles into the conversation. The father just said he left this sort of thing to his wife.

The psychologist then saw Charles by himself. Charles was nervous about being separated from his parents, but eventually allowed them to leave him in the room with the psychologist, who had particular experience in interviewing young children. Charles would not talk to her, but she eventually managed to encourage him to play with some family dolls. The way he played, especially with the female dolls, suggested to her that he was quite an angry boy. She was really unable to draw any other conclusions in this first interview.

She then saw the parents by themselves while Charles was looked after in the waiting area by a receptionist. She asked whether there was anything else the couple wanted to tell her that they had not wanted to say in front of Charles. It seemed as if the father might have something to say, but he seemed unable to *bring himself to do so. The psychologist said she thought that Charles really was suffering from depression and anxiety and that his pains were somehow linked to these feelings.*

Over the next three months the psychologist saw the family on several more occasions. She also worked with the school to monitor Charles's attendance there. A mixture of family sessions and individual therapy for Charles proved helpful. Father became more involved. Gradually Charles's pains became less frequent, he started to see his friends again and his school attendance became much more regular.

What Types of Treatment Are Provided and How Are They Selected?

The treatment the child needs will be chosen for a number of reasons. If there are stresses in school or the home that seem to be at the root of the problem, these will naturally be tackled first. When the problem is seen mainly as within the child, individual therapy of some type is likely to be the most important part of treatment. Where the problem is thought to be in the way family members interact, then family therapy will have more prominence. Other important considerations include the availability of particular treatment types and the sort of treatment with which the therapist is most experienced. If parents feel unhappy with the form of treatment they are offered, they should not hesitate to raise the matter with a member of the staff of the clinic or with their own doctor. The service should take such concerns seriously, whilst also bearing in mind the best treatment based on their understanding of the complete situation. Increasingly, brief methods of intervention are now employed in specialist services as first-line treatments.

At the start of this chapter, we talked about the 2019 NICE guidelines on the treatment of depression in children and young people. Part of the role of the NICE guidelines is to look at the evidence for different types of treatment, and suggest which ones are most likely to be helpful for different children. For children with a more mild depression, they suggest that most children can probably be helped by watchful waiting, or else some type of group intervention. NICE is very clear that antidepressant medication should not be used for the initial treatment of children and young people with mild depression.

When depression is more severe, however, NICE recommends that the professionals should make a careful assessment, and then talk with children and their families about the different types of therapy available, trying to make sure that they can meet each family's individual needs, preferences and values.

There are a number of talking therapies which have evidence of being helpful for children and young people with depression. It can sometimes be quite confusing to know what the difference is between them, so here we provide some information about the four most well-evidenced approaches: cognitive behavioural therapy

(CBT), systemic family therapy, psychodynamic (or psychoanalytic) psychotherapy, and interpersonal therapy (IPT). These four types of therapy are all recommended by NICE as treatments for child or adolescent depression. This doesn't mean that they will always help, or that other types of therapy aren't necessarily helpful – just that there isn't yet the high-quality research that demonstrates that other approaches can be effective.

Cognitive Behavioural Therapy (CBT)

Depression can also be seen as a disorder of thinking, and we have already described how some children and teenagers blame themselves when they have not done anything wrong. If we think we have done something wrong in the past, or that the future is hopeless, we may become depressed – our mood follows our thoughts. And if these ideas are false, our mood is inappropriate and undeserved. So, people who use cognitive therapy argue, helping a depressed child or teenager to think differently and more accurately about his or her past, present or future will also help lift the depression. CBT is about modifying negative thinking in order to improve the low mood such thinking produces.

How do CBT therapists, and they may be psychologists or psychiatrists, work? Often, the child is asked to explain what she or he means by words like 'angry', 'happy', 'worried', 'cheerful', 'sad' and 'depressed', and to give some examples of when she or he recently experienced these. The child is also asked to describe thoughts and ideas at the time of these experiences. Next, she or he may be asked to keep a diary of moods and the thoughts accompanying them. Following this, the child is asked to try to make links between thoughts and the moods that go with them. One or two tasks may then be set, and it is suggested that the child will feel happier when the task is accomplished.

The child will face difficult situations. It is suggested that she or he thinks of different solutions and chooses one of them. For example, one child may be faced with a bully at school and helped to choose whether to tell a teacher or parents, work out ways of avoiding the bully, talk to other children about ways of avoiding the bully, and so on. Another may be helped to examine whether ideas that people are against them or think little of them are accurate and encouraged to check such ideas against reality. Improved social relationships can be linked to improved mood states.

Specific techniques such as role play with the therapist can sometimes help to make change easier for the child. As time goes on, the child is encouraged to challenge previous assumptions that events around him or her have a negative significance. For example, a child may be helped to see that a mother's bad moods are not caused by the child's behaviour but have all sorts of other reasons. The core of the treatment involves self-monitoring and problem-solving at a conscious level.

Nowadays CBT can also be offered in a digital form. This is partly because in many parts of the country there aren't enough trained therapists to see all the young people who need help – it has been estimated that only about 25 per cent of children and young people who need a mental health specialist actually see one. Online and digital forms of CBT might also suit some young people, who may prefer to engage with something via an app than by going to a clinic. Some research suggests that computerised forms of CBT may be as helpful as face-to-face therapy for some young people, although not enough studies have been done yet to be sure about this.

Nadia was a fifteen-year-old girl who was first seen by a child and adolescent psychiatrist two days after she had been sent to an accident and emergency department, having swallowed twenty paracetamol tablets. She had had to have a stomach washout, had been very unwell, and had been lucky not to have suffered any permanent damage to her kidneys or liver. When the psychiatrist saw her, she was very tearful and upset. She explained to him that she had been feeling low for about four months, since she had had an attack of 'flu. Gradually she had become more and more depressed, not wanting to see her friends, hating school, sleeping poorly and being irritable with her parents and her younger sister. She felt people talked about her behind her back. She couldn't get out of her mind an episode about six months ago when she had been responsible for another girl being pushed out of her group of friends because of a row over a boy at the neighbouring school.

The psychiatrist saw Nadia's parents, who explained that they just didn't know what had been wrong with their daughter. She had been just so irritable over the previous few months that she had made life impossible for everybody. They had not known what to do for the best. Every time they had tried to talk to her she had snapped at them. They were appalled and ashamed that she had tried to end her life. It turned out that Nadia's father had himself been depressed for several months about six years ago, but he had not been irritable and it had not occurred to her parents that she might have the same problem. The psychiatrist took a full account of the problem from both Nadia and her parents and came to the conclusion that Nadia had a depressive illness.

Nadia was given antidepressant medication at the same time as she began a course of cognitive behavioural therapy. The psychological treatment aimed to help her to check on how realistic her thoughts were. She kept a diary noting when she thought people were talking about her and why she had come to this conclusion. She slowly improved both in her thinking and in her mood and became less irritable and depressed. Although Nadia had another bout of depression at university, she remained well for most of the time and was able to lead a very normal and enjoyable life for the rest of her school days and at university.

Psychodynamic (or Psychoanalytic) Psychotherapy

Child and adolescent psychotherapists take the view that much depression is caused by emotions and thoughts that the child or teenager finds difficult to bring to the surface. The psychotherapist helps children to explore what is going on for them through play, drawing or discussion. Although child psychotherapists will usually work with parents as well, for some children, changes within the family, or the lifting of pressures upon them, are not enough to help them overcome their complex feelings.

Psychotherapy looks not only at problem areas but at the child's whole personality and coping strategies. When a child is offered psychotherapy, the therapist and child meet one to one on a regular basis, often once a week or occasionally more often. This can help to build a safe therapeutic relationship. The child may be encouraged to find expression in playing with toys or in drawing. Often, however, especially with older children, treatment is entirely through talking.

The following examples show how two depressed boys had reacted quite differently to the development of diabetes. Both boys reacted against the diabetic treatment and would not become involved in planning either a diet or an insulin regime. Both became withdrawn and depressed, and their schoolwork deteriorated.

> *Steven was only interested in sport, both playing it and watching it. His increased activity led to further problems with control of his diabetes. During psychotherapy it emerged that he had great anxieties about the loss of control over his body. He felt that all the injections had damaged his body's ability to hold together – as if his skin was punctured all over and could not hold him in.*
>
> *Darren's worries were quite different. He was primarily concerned about feeling different from other people. He had particular difficulty in feeling that he could grow up to be an active and effective man, because he felt that he was so unlike his healthy father.*
>
> *Once these issues were uncovered and addressed in therapy, both boys were able to participate in control of their diabetes, their mood improved and they were able to settle down again to ordinary life.*

A depressed child will gradually develop a relationship with the therapist through play, drawing or talking. In this way, the therapist and child explore together how the child copes with life. The psychotherapist will help the child develop an understanding of his or her feelings, and how these affect behaviour and relationships. This may involve exploring how past experiences and relationships affect the child's ways of coping in the present. The therapist will not usually suggest solutions to children's difficulties, feeling that it is better for them to strengthen their own ability to reason and work out alternatives for themselves, rather than depend on the therapist. Psychotherapy is a gradual process during which children are allowed to explore their depression. It is particularly important in depression that angry and aggressive feelings which may arise are brought to the surface. It is a relief to the child to discover that these negative feelings can be tolerated and expressed. The therapist acknowledges what the child is going through, and this empathy and expression of feeling can bring relief. It enables the child to move on, psychologically, to discover new strengths and coping abilities.

The therapist will always keep family issues in mind and may work with another professional who will see the parents, and sometimes the family, while the child is in psychotherapy. Sometimes the therapist will do this job himself or herself.

Family Therapy

Sometimes people talk about childhood depression as being a problem located within the child, but this is not always the most helpful way to think about things. We know, for example, that parental problems, especially family discord, can have a big impact on young people's depression, and so sometimes it is important to go beyond offering help to the child or young person on their own. Family therapists would want to think about the whole family, not just the person who presents with problems. Family therapists view the problem a child brings as possibly serving a purpose for the family as a whole unit. Thus, a depressed child can be understood better within a set of family relationships, constantly acting upon each other in a circular way. In other words, the problem does not belong to the child, but to the family; and solutions often lie with the whole family, not just the child alone. The child is showing behaviour in relation to other family members.

> *Ian, aged twelve years and an only child, was brought to a clinic by his parents, who were worried and also exasperated by his depression, lack of interest in activities he previously enjoyed and feelings of hopelessness. His father did most of the talking, explaining how he had tried everything to bring his son out of himself. Ian's mother was silent, but the family therapist felt she was very angry, especially with her husband. It gradually became clear that Ian's father had been made redundant six months previously and was having no success in finding another job. He was spending much more time with Ian.*
>
> *Previously, Ian's mother had made all the decisions about her son, but now she felt pushed out. She had started to argue with her husband about the way he was taking Ian away from his friends to go fishing and to football matches with him. Ian had then*

started to say he did not want to go out at all. His father then criticised him, and his mother withdrew more.

When the situation became clear to the therapist and the parents it was possible for them to see how Ian's low mood was expressing a lot of feelings in the family that hadn't been clearly expressed or shared. Once the family began to see things this way, they were also able to argue less about Ian, and his depression lifted, although it did not disappear completely.

Family therapy usually takes the form of meetings with the entire family (or whoever it is felt, after discussion, should be involved) and a family therapist. These may be limited to an agreed number of sessions (often six to eight), or may be open-ended, over a longer period. Often, they occur at fortnightly intervals in order to permit the family to work on things at home between sessions.

Sometimes the meetings take place in a large room, one wall of which is a one-way mirror. The family therapist may have a co-worker or a team who will observe the session from behind this mirror-screen, in order to gain an independent perspective on the events taking place within the therapy room. The co-worker or a member of the team might sometimes come into the room to share their view. Some families find this very helpful, as they may get caught up in one way of seeing things, and this outside perspective can change how they see what is going on.

There are different kinds of family therapists, but most of them work through understanding and changing the way family members interact with each other. Very often, family trees are drawn during the family sessions, to help clarify just what the family tasks are at this stage of the children's lives. Each stage presents the family members with psychological and relationship tasks to perform. Family difficulties may arise at times of change. Other family members might have their own 'life-cycle issues', which will all interact within the family unit. For example, family life changes when a teenager begins working towards greater independence and eventually leaves home. The family as a whole is affected. Relationships between the parents will be affected; they have to look to their future as a couple again as their children leave. Loss may be central to the whole family's functioning and may be associated with grandparents becoming elderly or dying.

One of the advantages of family therapy is that it allows for improved communication, especially when family members have issues they find difficult to talk about without help. The therapist will therefore be particularly interested to hear family members who have difficulty in making their thoughts and feelings known.

Some parents are worried they will be blamed for their child's problem. But family therapy is not interested in 'blame' and not necessarily concerned with causes but works by understanding just how the family is working together; and how the family might want to work together differently. The whole family is affected by a child's depression and can in turn affect the resolution of it.

Sometimes a multifamily approach may be offered, which means that the therapist will bring together several families, who perhaps all share certain difficulties. These meetings might include some psychoeducation, but families might also be invited to work together to try to address some of the problems that brought them to seek help.

Interpersonal Psychotherapy (IPT)

What happens in our interpersonal relationships and how we feel are closely linked. For example, when we have problems in our relationships, this can make us feel sad. And when sadness deepens into feeling depressed, we might also feel tired and go out less, which can create a distance between us and the people we are close to. IPT is a well-researched form of therapy, which helps young people to recognise these two-way links between their interpersonal relationships and their depressive symptoms. It then helps them to improve their relationships in order to reduce their symptoms of depression.

IPT is normally conducted over twelve weekly sessions with the young person and three additional sessions with parents. In the first four sessions, the therapist and the young person talk about the young person's experience of depression and the network of relationships in the young person's life, focusing mainly on current relationships or those that may have changed recently. This helps them to work out the best things to work on in the rest of the therapy, typically focusing on significant changes, conflicts, bereavements or difficulties making or maintaining relationships.

Group Therapy

In some clinics, children are sometimes treated together in groups of roughly the same age. They may be mixed in terms of gender, although sometimes they are single-gender groups. There will be one or two therapists present.

The group may be based on a CBT approach, in which case it will probably be focused on a particular subject, with a set agenda; or it may be less directive and have an open agenda. Group leaders may direct the children into specific activities, aiming to work on particular issues such as cooperation and sharing, or they may let the children decide on the activity and issues together. Sometimes video is used to help the children observe themselves in order to encourage change. In those cases, written permission from the parents is necessary.

Such groups usually meet once a week or fortnightly. They may run over a short number of agreed sessions or be more open-ended, depending on the way the group itself develops to decide duration or content.

Antidepressant Medication

There is some research showing that antidepressant medication may be helpful; however, the NICE guidelines recommend that such medication shouldn't be offered on its own to children with depression. It should usually be offered alongside some kind of talking therapy, or when talking therapies have been tried and are not helping.

When the problems of a child or adolescent are at least moderately severe and do not respond to 'talking' treatments, a doctor, usually a child and adolescent psychiatrist, will consider the possible use of medication. When this happens, it is important that the doctor speaks to you, and your child, about why they are suggesting this, and explains about possible side effects, including any long-term effects, and also what might happen when your child wants to stop taking the medication. As the information can be quite detailed, they should provide written information as well and give you and your child an opportunity to ask any questions you have. Parents, children and young people are often very scared about taking medication, and it is important that such feelings are discussed and taken into account when deciding whether to use antidepressants. One important aim of prescribing medication is to improve mood to a point where talking therapies become more possible than they would otherwise be. One fifteen-year-old, who had improved from a depressive state after treatment combining psychotherapy with medication, put it this way:

'Therapy was really good, and it helped and probably medication as well, but that was more about the lack of safety blanket until I was feeling better. I think the main thing was the therapy – just finding different methods for coping. But I knew that if things did go downhill again I could just go back on medication.' (Fatima, 15)

The main antidepressants used in children and young people are selective serotonin reuptake inhibitors (SSRIs), which have been used since the 1980s. These have fewer side effects and are generally reckoned to be more effective and safer than the older antidepressants (tricyclic antidepressants) because of a lower risk of serious harm in the case of an overdose. They do have side effects, although these are mainly minor, and usually (but not always) wear off after a couple of weeks. In 2003, it became clear that a very small number of young people became more suicidal or had increased self-harm after starting SSRIs. Since then, doctors have been advised to be more cautious about prescribing them, and families are warned of this possible side effect.

All the same, many child and adolescent psychiatrists think, on the basis of their experience, that these drugs can be helpful, sometimes very helpful, when serious depression is present. If tablets are prescribed, they need to be taken regularly and, if they are effective, they usually need to be continued for at least six months.

The main SSRI used for depression is fluoxetine. Sometimes other SSRIs such as sertraline or citalopram are used if fluoxetine does not work. Although these medicines are called antidepressants, they also work for anxiety disorders and obsessive-compulsive disorder, so may be prescribed for these conditions. Occasionally, psychiatrists will prescribe other antidepressants such as mirtazapine or vortioxetine. Another form of medication, lithium carbonate, is used very occasionally in older children and teenagers who have marked mood swings (see earlier section on psychotic depression in Chapter 1). This medication, which is used to prevent attacks of depression, has to be carefully monitored. The teenager has to have regular blood checks to make sure the level of lithium is kept within certain limits.

With all these forms of medication, it is important to make sure tablets are kept well out of the way of a teenager who might be suicidal. Of course, that also applies to tablets taken by other members of the household. It is best to keep all tablets locked away, particularly if there are toddlers around, who may mistake them for sweets.

Conclusion

It can sometimes feel a bit overwhelming trying to access child mental health services, and to make sense of all the different treatments that are talked about as possibly helpful for your child's depression. As no two children are alike, there is no one approach that works for everyone, and sometimes you may need to try several things before finding what works best for your child.

If you are dealing with doctors, psychiatrists, nurses or psychotherapists, it is important that you feel able to ask them as many questions as you want, and to make sure that they answer your questions clearly. Knowing why a particular treatment is being recommended is important. You'll also want to know what the evidence is to support that treatment, and what the risks are in taking that approach. It is also important to discuss with them what will happen if the treatment isn't working, and what other choices you and your child have.

Don't worry if you have to ask people to explain things several times. Supporting your child when they are suffering from depression can be hard work, and it is important that you find support for yourself as well. But help is out there, and we hope this book has given you some understanding of the many things you can do to make a difference.

Last Words – from a Parent

We thought there was something wrong because he was unhappy – he's normally a very happy cheery boy, outgoing, wants to be with friends, playing with friends. But he didn't want to see his friends, even on weekends, for example, when he was able to, he didn't want to. And just looking down and, you know we talk quite often, but there would be lots of tears and that was not like him at all. So, we realised that something was very, very different.

We didn't really understand where it was coming from. You know maybe it's puberty or thinking about exams and that sort of thing . . . At the time we knew he needed help, to help him grapple with the various things that he was feeling – but combining that with, we were hoping for some sort of practical measures that could help him to cope, more short term. I mean, there was still some question as to whether he should have some medication or not and I think, you know, we had some reservations and concerns about that. So, we talked to our GP, and luckily she was quite good at recognising he needed help, and referred him to [a child and adolescent mental health service]. It was difficult because it took a while before he was seen, but he was offered therapy, and they talked to us about medication too.

We had concerns that therapy would stir up strong feelings he wouldn't be able to cope with – but I don't think that happened. I'm not able to evaluate how much impact the therapy had – sometimes you just don't know until afterwards . . . but it was the only thing that got him up and out of the house – we never had to say, 'Come on, you've got to go' – to me that was important . . . And sometimes out of the blue he would say on the way home, 'Oh, you know, da da da', and it was clear that it was a follow-on to what he'd been discussing in therapy. So maybe it gave him the breathing space to think and reflect . . .

He's made a lot of progress since then – more energy, definitely . . . more like his old self – making jokes, started working a bit, getting back into school. His energy level is much better. He's certainly not in the dark place where he was . . . He can now say 'this is upsetting me' or 'that makes me angry' – he's able to analyse some of his feelings.

Thinking back to that time when it all started, we were sort of struggling and didn't quite understand, you know, understand him, and . . . it was quite difficult for all of us. But now we sort of know where his thinking and his understanding is, and mentally where he's at. It's much easier for us all. Things aren't perfect – but I think we're going to be OK.

Chapter

8

Message to Governments

Although this is a book primarily for parents, we think it right to point out that there is a great deal that governments could do to make it easier for parents and teachers to help children avoid emotional problems. The policy measures we list below would help parents, teachers and children themselves reduce the frequency of clinical depression in the young. Perhaps some parents might use their influence and their votes to bring about changes in these directions.

- Reduce poverty. Parents who do not know how they are going to put food on the table will find it much more difficult to attend to the emotional needs of their children.
- Increase the availability of programmes for preschool children in order that young children can receive appropriate stimulation and problems can be detected earlier.
- Cut the number of public examinations to reduce academic stress.
- Enhance the status of relationship and sex education so that children and young people are better informed and so will find porn sites less appealing.
- Encourage school inspectors, like OFSTED, to give greater credit to schools that promote social inclusion policies involving black, Asian and minority ethnic groups, children with disabilities and LGBT students; and that promote emotional well-being and work hard to reduce bullying.
- Give greater resources to schools to enable them to provide more art and music in the curriculum, and to timetable curriculum space for personal development and self-care, so as to encourage emotional expressiveness in the young.
- Increase out-of-school youth provision, to keep young people off the streets and provide them with positive social activities.
- Give real parity to physical and mental health, by ensuring that all children with mental health difficulties can access appropriate support in a timely way.

Resources and Further Reading

Useful Organisations and Websites

The 'On My Mind' section of the Anna Freud Centre website has a lot of useful information for young people and parents, including the 'Youth Wellbeing Directory', which gives up-to-date contact details about local services for children and young people across the United Kingdom, including Child and Adolescent Mental Health Services (CAMHS). The website also includes a 'Jargon Buster' section, information about self-care, as well as guides to understanding referrals and treatment. www.annafreud.org/on-my-mind/

A group of parents also made a short film with the Anna Freud Centre about caring for a teenager with depression: 'Journey Through the Shadows', which can be found on YouTube.

All the organisations listed below provide information and advice, and some have helplines. We have given website addresses where we think they are available, but we cannot take responsibility for their content.

NHS Online

www.nhs.uk/

The NHS website has a lot of useful information about living well, including guidance about diet, sleep, etc. The 'care and support' section of the website also provides lots of information about NHS services, including Child and Adolescent Mental Health Services.

One part of the website, the 'Moodzone', includes information for parents of anxious and depressed children:

www.nhs.uk/conditions/stress-anxiety-depression/anxiety-in-children/

Young Minds

https://youngminds.org.uk/find-help/for-parents/

Parents helpline: 0808 802 5544

Publishes a number of relevant information sheets, including *Parents Survival Guide* and *Parents Guide to Support A–Z*, and has online information about supporting a child with depression.

Childline

Confidential helpline for children and young people; Freepost NATN 1111, London E1 6BR

Helpline: 0800 1111 (24 hours, free) www.childline.org.uk

Family Lives (formerly Parent Line)

Informative website and confidential helpline for parents; Helpline: 0808 800 2222 (24 hours, free)

Textphone: 0800 783 6783 (for people with speech or hearing impairments, 9.00 am to 5.00 pm, Monday to Friday, free).

www.familylives.org.uk

Royal College of Psychiatrists

4, Prescot Street, London, E1 8BB

Useful information about childhood depression: www.rcpsych.ac.uk/mental-health/parents-and-young-people/young-people/depression-in-children-and-young-people-for-young-people

Kooth

Online support for young people with mental health problems.

www.kooth.com/

Young Stonewall

Information and advice for LGBT children and young people.

www.youngstonewall.org.uk/

Muslim Youth Helpline

Helpline providing culturally sensitive support to Muslim youth under the age of 25.

0808 808 2008

www.myh.org.uk

NSPCC

The NSPCC Helpline provides advice and support to adults who are concerned about the safety or welfare of a child.

0808 800 5000

www.nspcc.org.uk

Women's Aid

National charity working to end domestic violence against women and children. Freephone 24-hr National Domestic Violence Helpline 0808 2000 247

www.womensaid.org.uk/

Respect

This is a UK membership association for domestic violence perpetrator programmes and associated support services. Helpline for perpetrators: 0808 802 4040 (free from landlines and most mobiles).

The Hideout

Women's Aid have created this space to help children and young people understand domestic abuse, and how to take positive action if it's happening to you.
https://thehideout.org.uk/

The Samaritans

24-hour service offering confidential emotional support to anyone who is in crisis. Helpline 08457 909090 (UK), 1850 609090 (ROI); e-mail: jo@samaritans.org

Office of National Statistics (ONS)

Finally, for those who wish to know the facts about the frequency of depression in children and young people, the ONS publishes results of authoritative population surveys. At the time of writing, the most recent, published in 2017, is available on
https://digital.nhs.uk/data-and-information/publications/statistical/mental-health-of-children-and-young-people-in-england

Further Reading

If you'd like to read more about healthy child development or childhood depression, or about approaches to parenting, you may find these books of interest:

Sam Cartwright-Hatton (2007) *Coping with an Anxious or Depressed Child*. London: Oneworld Publications.

Sheila Redfern and Alistair Cooper (2015) *Reflective Parenting: A Guide to Understanding What's Going on in Your Child's Mind*. London: Routledge.

Margot Waddell (2005) *Understanding 12–14-Year-Olds*. London: Jessica Kingsley Publishers.

Margot Waddell (2018) *On Adolescence*. London: Jessica Kingsley Publishers.

Index